Living
a Loved Life

Praise for *Living a Loved Life*

"When we learn to love the life we are living, the joke is on us. We have been inhabitants of Paradise all along. Who knew? Modern neuroscience is catching on to the ancient wisdom that Dawna—and her preternaturally wise grandmother—transmit with such grace through luminous stories that ring the doorbell of the heart. When we savor what is and find possibility in life's inevitable challenges, our nervous system is reprogrammed from self-protection to sweet connection with the astonishing miracle of life."

—Joan Borysenko, PhD, *New York Times* bestselling author of *Minding the Body, Mending the Mind*

"I love this book. After reading it, I'm inspired to be a grandfather but also an elder. I wish I had a chance to meet Dawna's grandmother…but I think I already have…because, as Dawna wrote, 'she passed into me.' Now her grandmother has passed into me too, and I can use all the help I can get!"

—Al Carey, CEO emeritus of PepsiCo North America and chairman of Unifi Inc.

"I'm sure I'm not alone in my life-long yearning for a gramma who was wise, taught me the most important life lessons, who adored me, and whose 'believing eyes' would bring forward my gifts for the world. Dawna Markova, in her touching book, *Living a Loved Life*, is kind enough to loan her exquisite grandmother to us to reaffirm that which is necessary for each of us to live life in its depth and fullness."

—Linda Bloom, co-author of *101 Things I Wish I Knew When I Got Married: Simple Lessons to Make Love Last*

"Internationally renowned thought leader and personal growth expert Dawna Markova, PhD, brings us *Living a Loved Life* which challenges us to listen to the heartfelt lessons necessary to create the most loving life possible. She inspires us with stories and keen insights into discovering our truest purpose on earth. Her teachings reflect the wisdom of our elders and empowers us to live a fuller life. In her irresistible, poetic narrative style, the author insightfully shares how it is possible to braid our strengths from even our most difficult life lessons. Her teachings guide us to reclaim our voice, redefine our story, and create the life of our dreams. Buy this insightful book today and gift it to everyone you care about. It's a rare jewel and a life-affirming literary masterpiece."

—Robyn Spizman, author of *Loving Out Loud: The Power of a Kind Word*, media personality, and *New York Times* bestselling author

"Dawna Markova is one of the great wisdom teachers of our time. She touched countless lives with *I Will Not Die an Unlived Life*, and many more will be touched by *Living a Loved Life*. This beautifully written book was shaped by three questions: 'How do I find a way to live a life I can love now? How do I help make it possible for those who will come after me to do the same? How do I re-collect the wisdom earned through my own and others' challenges?' I don't know anyone who would not benefit from exploring those questions, especially in the company of a master mentor, a true companion on the journey toward the human possibility. That's Dawna Markova, and this book is her gift to you and me."

—Parker J. Palmer, author of *On the Brink of Everything, Let Your Life Speak, Healing the Heart of Democracy, and The Courage to Teach*

Living
a Loved Life

Awakening Wisdom Through Stories of
Inspiration, Challenge, and Possibility

Dawna Markova, PhD

Mango Publishing

CORAL GABLES

For permission requests, please contact the publisher at:
Mango Publishing Group
2850 S Douglas Road, 2nd Floor
Coral Gables, FL 33134 USA
info@mango.bz

For special orders, quantity sales, course adoptions and corporate sales, please
email the publisher at sales@mango.bz. For trade and wholesale sales, please
contact Ingram Publisher Services at customer.service@ingramcontent.com or
+1.800.509.4887.

Living a Loved Life: Awakening Wisdom Through Stories of Inspiration, Challenge,
and Possibility

Library of Congress Cataloging-in-Publication number: 2019948614
ISBN: (print) 978-1-64250-126-1, (ebook) 978-1-64250-127-8
BISAC category code BODY, MIND & SPIRIT / Inspiration & Personal Growth

Printed in the United States of America

Blessing

To David Adam Peck

These stories are my heirlooms and your inheritance. They are the true wealth that I have to pass on to you. Consider this my last will and testament, because it will take all of my will to finish it and it is a testament to the wisdom that has carried me forward through many challenges. Passing it on to you will enable me to release my last breath with deep satisfaction.

To all those who yearn to love the life they are living.

Table of Contents

~

Yeasting

"

"It's all a question of story. We are in trouble now because we do not have a good story. The Old Story sustained us for a long period of time. It shaped our emotional attitudes, provided us with life purpose, energized action. It consecrated suffering, integrated knowledge, guided education. We awoke in the morning and knew where we were. We could answer the questions of our children. We could identify crime, punish criminals. Everything was taken care of because the story was there. It did not make men good or make for unfailing warmth in human association. But it did provide a context in which life could function in a meaningful manner. Now we are between stories."

—Thomas Berry

How Do I Live a Loved Life?

The coauthor of this book is a ghost. My grandmother was a midwife and healer. She sat with people as they entered the world and as they left it. She never set foot in a school and could neither read nor write. I haven't included her name on the title page because I never really knew what it was. I just called her "Grandma." Others called her "Ma" or "Dora," or by her husband's name, "Michael's wife," as if she were his possession.

As I am writing about her to you, she becomes alive again: a tiny woman with a fierce will. In the late 1800s, she ran across Russian potato fields to escape Cossack soldiers who had killed her first two children and brother during a pogrom, an attack on Jewish villages. She and my grandfather escaped to New York by boat, traveling in steerage. Driven by that indomitable will to foster life, she gave birth to eight more children in a two-bedroom apartment on the fifth floor of an old brick tenement in Hell's Kitchen.

One of her feet was planted on the spiritual side and the other on the pragmatic. But to talk about her in terms of one side or the other is inaccurate, because Grandma was always braiding together people, their resources, and the challenges of their lives so that they would be inspired to love their existence. Her prayers went something like this: "May Willie's ability to make money help Sammy, who has to sleep in a cold car because he can't afford to pay his rent. May they both love the life they are living. May they each live the life they love."

On the day when I am writing these words, the whole world seems to be teetering on a knife edge between right/wrong, either/or, us/them. I have been asking myself several evocative questions for the past two years. They have midwifed the pages you are now reading: How do I find a way to live a life I can love? How do I help make it possible for those who will come after me to do the same? What do I need to remember, as in "re-member," to bring together all that has been torn in two? How do I re-collect the wisdom earned through my own and others' challenges? What is the most effective way to pass it on? Is there a place inside me and between us where vanished wisdom secretly gathers?

My grandmother gave me one of the greatest gifts one person can give to another: she helped me to discover how my life matters. She told me that the moment I was born, Life made a Promise to the world that only I could fulfill. She inspired my search for what this could be by telling me stories of her own experiences and by asking me wide-open questions that would lead me to live a life I would love.

When people don't believe their lives really matter, they shrug, feel impotent, and disconnect from one another, slowly declining into what they most despise. Grandma used to kiss the unique marks at the very ends of my fingertips, calling them "promise prints." She said they prove that never before and never again will there be another such as me.

Understanding how each of us does and can matter is the most powerful force I know to make it possible for a human being to love his or her existence. Why don't most of us know this? So many of the people I have worked with for the past fifty years didn't. Whether it was as a psychotherapist helping groups of people heal sexual abuse and couples repair the ruptures between them, or as an advisor to CEOs and senior leadership teams, one person after another told me that deep down in the canyons of their bones, they felt as if their lives didn't really matter. Why isn't this lack obvious to us? Why don't we know how to instill a sense of personal significance in our children and grandchildren so they can love being alive?

I believe there are three implicit forces that contribute to this:

1. The current dismissal and dishonoring of elders and their importance to the rest of us has resulted in this awareness being eclipsed. In many traditions, elders were the ones who pointed out a basic fact of human life to the youngest members of a community: that the fingerprints at the end of our reach prove that each of us is a one-of-a-kind marvel that has never existed before and never will again.

2. Our educational and cultural systems are *deficit focused*—in other words, attention is solely focused on what doesn't work and what is wrong rather than on what does work and has worked (i.e., "You got four wrong on your spelling test" rather than, "You got twenty-six right.") Consequently, it is rare to find someone who is as articulate about the talents they have to contribute as about the flaws they need to hide or improve.

3. A major thinking strategy embedded in Western culture is domination rather than collaboration. What has been honored and respected, therefore, is power over rather than power with others. What makes this possible is culturally inculcating the belief that some people's thinking (and existence) is more important than others. If you can dismiss the contribution of a person frequently enough, he or she will shrug and believe that because they can't have an effect on an outcome, they don't matter. Conversely, if you create collaborative conditions whereby the stories of each person's life experiences and the resources embedded in them can

be evoked and respected, both the individual and collective intellectual capital is increased, as is a deeper understanding of how each of us matters to the rest of us. It is this that makes it possible to love the life you are living.

I am a midwife as my grandmother was, but of possibilities within and between people. I've lived many incarnations in the past seven decades: as a teacher, psychotherapist, researcher, and organizational fairy godmother. When I have to fill out a form that asks for my occupation, I write "professional thinking partner." The Latin root of the word "professional" is *profere*, meaning to profess faith. I profess my faith by being present with others in such a way that what was broken can be made whole again. When I think in partnership with someone, I listen deeply enough to hear the question his or her life is asking. I am constantly wondering how to make connections within and between the best of a person and the challenges he or she is facing. Stories then rise in my mind, stories that synthesize, connect, and widen the horizon each is facing. It feels like a great melting, as if Life is saying, "Yes!" to and through me.

I also write books as a way of fumbling through this endless path of confusion we call a human life. Most of the ones I have written are rooted in a lifelong curiosity about thinking. In graduate school, I did research in cognitive psychology and intellectual diversity. None of that rational training helped much, though, with the personal relational and physical challenges of abuse, divorce, and cancer. My mind broke apart with questions that no one could answer: "How can I love this life while living with a 'terminal' disease? What will balance all the random acts of violence that are happening to and around me? What's unfinished for me to give? What difference have I made—and what difference can I make—in a world that seems to be growing crazier and more chaotic by the hour?" Since I couldn't

answer them, these questions opened my mind to a state of wonder.
And it was wonder and the stories that emerged from it which led
me to discover the Promise of my life.

Grandma taught me that there is both perspective and wisdom
hidden in our greatest difficulties. They can help us realize how we
matter as well as what really matters to us. I learned from her that
certain unanswerable questions can encourage one's mind to open
and to wander like a kite in a wind, noticing what emerges rather
than struggling helplessly to find a single answer on which to land
in certainty. When I have done this, what often bubbles up is a story
about something I've experienced. I have woven these stories with
those of others into several books: *Random Acts of Kindness*, *Spot of
Grace*, and *I Will Not Die an Unlived Life*.

I didn't know where the ideas for any of those books really came
from. I had no idea anyone would want to read them. Winter in
Vermont can be extremely stormy. When I first moved there, I
frequently had to tie a rope to the back of the old farmhouse where
I lived so my six-year-old son David and I could find our way to the
barn in the blinding snow, feed the horse, and then find our way
home again. The books I wrote were also a kind of rope to which I
clung through the twin storms of losing my father and my diagnosis
of terminal cancer.

In 1999, I withdrew to a tiny cabin on a snowy mountaintop to
explore how to love the life that remained. Once more I turned
my grief to ink in order to find my way through this storm of
unanswerable questions. I had no intention of anyone else reading
the words I scribbled. I was just writing myself home. In three
months, I realized that I had written a book to help me explore
the most essential questions I couldn't answer: How do I live a life
I can love? How do I love the life I am living? I was habituated to

questions I could answer. But *these* questions couldn't be answered, and something very different emerged in my mind. They lifted me and carried me beyond the image of myself that I had been holding onto so tightly. They floated me to a place beyond right or wrong, into an ocean of inner resources, stories, and wisdom that I hadn't even imagined existed. I came to understand that when faced with a grand challenge, as I was then and as we all are now, there is also a call to live from everything that is within you.

Six months after I withdrew to the cabin, the questions and stories that had emerged were published as a book, *I Will Not Die an Unlived Life: Discovering Passion and Purpose*, with a poem I had written after my father died printed on the back cover.

I began to get letters and emails from people who told me how much the poem had helped them. That wasn't my intent. I just wanted to learn how to love the life I was living and what changes I had to make so I could create a life I could love. Twenty years later, it is rare that a day goes by without one of those letters arriving either as an email or in my mailbox. A woman in New Mexico wrote an opera based on the poem, and a Canadian artist created a huge oil painting which now hangs in a Toronto museum. A woman in South Africa, Nomathembe Luhabe, took the poem all over her country and read it to crowds of people as she helped grow Nelson Mandela's movement to liberate their country. In 2004, she called me from Cape Town and said there was someone on the phone who wanted to ask me a question. In a deep resonant voice, Mandela asked, "What do you think the connection is between grief and the passion it takes to live a loved life?"

A year later, the Dalai Lama invited me to come to Dharamsala to meet him. He told me how the poem and the book had touched him deeply and asked me to sign his well-worn copy. My tears had indeed turned to ink. Inspired by an illiterate man born to an illiterate mother, the poem, carrying the transformative question, "How can I love the life I am living?" has circled the globe, appearing in places as far-flung as South America, China, Mexico, and Minnesota. Seeming strangers tell me a copy of it has been hanging over their desks for years, carrying them forward. The seed my father planted in my mother has indeed gone on to blossom and, through me, to fruit.

In these dark and fragmented Humpty Dumpty times, at a moment in history when possibility seems eclipsed and all the King's horses and all the King's men have convinced so many people that they can't and don't make a difference, I feel a great sorrow that so much innate talent and valuable life experience is undiscovered, untapped, and unloved. I long to inspire you who are reading these words to search for the reservoir of wisdom and capacity within you waiting to be discovered and shared with the rest of us. I know it is exactly the glue that can connect and help us create a possible world for those who will follow.

My grandmother didn't pass away from me, she passed into me. She saw things in people that they didn't recognize in themselves. When I was born, she looked at the palms of my tiny hands and realized that I was the one of all her grandchildren to whom she would pass on what she had learned. She told my father to bring me to her every Friday so she could teach me to birth possibility in people. He must have rolled his sky-blue eyes and shaken his head, as all of her children did at her "old country superstitions," but her will was stronger than his. For the first fourteen years of my life, he drove me to Hell's Kitchen every Friday morning to be with her.

As far as I know, there is not one other living person on this planet now who has felt her warm dry lips place kisses at the end of each fingertip. There is no one who remembers her faded yellow apron with tiny red roses or who tasted the end slice of the golden bread she baked every Friday. There's also no one else alive who sat next to her on the rusty fire escape outside her living room, listening to the whispery wisdom that emerged from her lips. It has nourished me in the leanest of moments. It has been sliced and served to friends, family, students, and every person with whom I have worked. They have licked the butter off their chin and said, "I wish I had a grandmother like yours." I kept promising them that someday I would write a book about her. Now I, too, am an old lady. If I don't serve her wisdom to you on these clean white pages, it will be lost forever. I once asked her why she kept teaching me each week. She replied simply, "So I can share my zava'ah with you," as if that should explain everything. Since no one in my family spoke much Hebrew, the word stored itself in the dark recesses of my unconscious mind until a few weeks ago, when it emerged in a dream where she was giving me a purple T-shirt. Emblazoned across the front in gold letters was the word "Zava'ah." The next morning, I leapt out of bed and looked up its meaning: "An ethical will describing the moral and spiritual understandings accumulated within a life. It is meant to be passed on to one's descendants in order to impart wisdom and inspiration from one generation to the next." I was elated as I realized that the book you are now reading is both her zava'ah and my own, a distillation of wisdom gathered as each of us searched to live lives we could love by fulfilling our Promise and making a difference in challenging times.

Because this book is essentially both Grandma's and my own zava'ah, we've shaped the stories the way she shaped her challah, a Sabbath bread. Each of its nine braids was yeasted by a question I asked her so I could discover how I matter. The first strand of each braid is a story formed from one of her teaching tales. It is written in the present tense so she can come alive for you. The second strand incorporates a personal challenge with which I struggled while trying to weave her wisdom into my life. The third story folds that wisdom into the current context through a narrative about someone I worked with as a thinking partner who was searching for how he or she could live a life they could love. After the loaf is braided, there are some evocative questions so that you can share them with those in your world.

This loaf of a book is created the way Grandma made her challah: yeasting, rising, kneading, braiding, baking, and sharing, because bread, gluten-free or otherwise, is the staff of life, basic to human nourishment. During World War II, there was a group of abandoned children in London who were gathered off the streets and taken to an orphanage. Most of them had been without love, caring, and nourishment for months. In the shelter, they were clothed, fed, and held. But there was a problem—they could not fall asleep. No matter what the caregivers told them, they didn't believe there would be food to eat in the morning. No matter what they did, the children insisted on staying awake. One night, a nurse had an idea. After tucking the kids into bed, she placed a slice of bread into each child's hand. Without fail, every one of them fell deeply asleep. Knowing they would awaken with nourishment to fill their bellies, the children could rest.

The discovery of how you live a life you love can be found hidden in the stories you tell about that life. Grandma and I are reaching out to you with wide-open questions and with slices of our own stories in the hope that they will yeast the Promise inside you. The inspiration we offer in the pages that follow is not in the questions or stories themselves, but rather in your encounter with them.

My coauthor says that if you never knew your grandparents or didn't like them, it's not a problem. She invites you to adopt her as your own. We are, after all, in this together. Each of us can be involved in the dance of spiraling generations in which the elders empower the young with their wisdom and the young empower the old with the energy of new possibility. Whether you are an "old soul" in a millennial body or an elder yourself, I pass the blessing of wisdom from her hands through mine into yours.

Rising

"

"The spiritual journey is an endless process of engaging life as it is, stripping away our illusions about ourselves, our world, and the relationship of the two, moving closer to reality as we do".

—Parker Palmer

What Was the Promise Life Made to the World the Moment You Were Born?

Grandma raises my open palm to her lips. I look at the little lines carved into the skin around them, wondering if they are there because she has spent so many moments of her life kissing things. She looks into my brown-green eyes with her brown-green eyes and whispers in a secret voice, "Did you know that there is a river of blood that runs right beneath your skin?"

My jaw drops open like a baby bird waiting for something delicious to fall in. I shake my head.

"Not only that," she continues, "but there are special gifts and prayers for you from all those who came before that are being carried in that river."

I know what prayers are because she told me she prayed for people whenever she made bread, but gifts floating in a bloody river? What does she mean?

"All of your grandparents and their grandparents and their grandparents before them dreamt that someday there would be one such as you: one who was free, well-fed, and smart because she could go to school and learn many wonderful things. They left their wisdom floating downstream in that river, the things Life had taught them. All of that is in your blood."

My mind unfolds its wings and lifts off my bones as I imagine those old people wrapping prayers and presents in bright boxes that float now in the red bloody river under my skin.

She places tiny flower petal kisses on the tips of my fingers, and then whispers, "And here there is something else even more special. No one else who has ever lived has marks like these, and no one else ever will. They prove you are unique, one-of-a kind, a miracle!" She pauses long enough for me to absorb what she's saying and then continues in a powdery voice, "Some people call them fingerprints, but truly they are promise prints. The moment you were born, Life made a Promise to the world. It left these marks at the very end of your fingers to help you remember to reach out and find what that promise is and make it real."

The next question falls out of my mouth all by itself. "So what is my Promise, Grandma? Tell me, tell me."

This time she kisses the tip of her own index finger, and then places it on the center of my forehead. "I can't tell you that, my darling. No one can. It's a great and wonderful mystery that you have to discover for yourself."

"But how will I do that, Grandma, and how will I know if I find the real Promise? And does everybody have a Promise, and—"

Her finger floats to my lips as she responds, "Those are wonderful questions, Ketzaleh (little kitten). You'll have to search for that Promise many, many years, asking big, wide questions. Life will reveal it to you by giving you clues and bringing many wise people into your world. Those people will tell stories that will help you feel more alive. Pay attention the way you do to riddles, because they can lead you forward."

We're standing in her kitchen next to the window where sunshine pours in on a table covered with shiny red oilcloth. Her gnarled fingers turn an oversized glass bowl upside down, and a mound of newly risen golden bread dough plops out. She slaps it down hard and says, "This is what the world does to you sometimes. It slaps you into shape, pushes you around, stretches you. This can make the talents you bring even stronger, Ketzaleh. The yeast in the dough is like the Promise that wants those talents to rise and reach out to others." As her fingers knead the dough firmly, she insists, "You must not give up. Keep searching for that Promise and for people that will help it rise again. There are forces and choices that flatten life and those that grow and inspire it."

I can't wait another minute, so I ask, "Grandma, will the wise people tell me what my Promise is? Do I have to make bread every Friday like you do to find it?"

She wipes her hands on the apron and covers the bowl with a yellow checked dishtowel. As I push it back into the sunny spot, she says, "My Promise is like the bread, Ketzaleh. I sit with people helping them be born. I do what I can to help the Life Force, the yeast, rise and take form. Your Promise is more like the bowl. That's all I can tell you now."

"My Promise is like a bowl?"

"Yes, like a bowl that will shatter when challenged. You need to learn how to mend the Bowl of Life so it is stronger than before to realize the Promise inside you."

The questions in my mind push out of my lips. "One more question, Grandma, just one. I'm sorry to keep asking, but I have to know— what happens after I find the Promise and keep it, then what?"

She turns to me, holding each of my cheeks in her warm palms and looking with infinite patience into the mirrors of my eyes. "You never have to apologize for your questions, dear one. Risk reaching for them, risk following them. As for what happens after you live out the Promise, well, by then, you'll be an old wise woman. Your prayers, your dreams, your gifts will flow beyond you into the River of Life so it can touch whoever comes after you."

Pretending I'm Not Pretending

In high school, I perfected the art of the shrug. The thing I said the most often was, "I'm bored." I had skipped a grade twice in elementary and middle school, and, at fifteen, the last thing I wanted was to stand out as special in any way. I was a flat-chested senior who still hadn't gotten her period. I figured out how to dumb myself down by simplifying my vocabulary and putting enough wrong answers on tests so that I could maintain a C average. But I was bored, bored all the way down to my bone marrow. All I wanted was to be left alone under the blankets with a flashlight or in my school locker, reading anything and everything I could find.

I decided my salvation would come in college. My mother and father both thought it was a waste of time, but I convinced them that I'd just be moping around the house and driving them crazy if I didn't go. They finally agreed, but only if I studied something that could lead to finding a husband: nursing would be best because it would expose me to a lot of doctors. Teaching was second-best, because I'd at least learn how to prepare for motherhood. Morton Barron, my high school counselor, suggested that, since I had a straight C average, the only safe school that I could get into was Syracuse University. I followed his "guidance," because at least it would take me away from boredom.

Of course, first I had to take the College Board exams. Unfettered by the need to dumb myself down, I surfed right through the waves of questions easily. A few weeks later, Morton Barron called me back into his office to ask how I had managed to cheat on the College Boards. I had no idea what he was talking about, so I just shrugged. He explained that I had earned virtually perfect scores on all the tests and that no girl with a straight C average could do that. He

insisted I take them again. A week after I did so, he called me back
and said the results were exactly the same. Maybe I hadn't cheated,
he conceded, but it was too late to apply to a better school, perfect
scores or not. My mother became concerned that no prince would
want a wife who was smarter than he. My father looked around the
721-acre campus of Syracuse with its tens of thousands of diverse
students and knew his little princess was going to be lost.

Which I was, of course. Lost, and still bored, bored, bored. In
education classes, they taught me how to draw Easter bunnies and
put swabs of cotton on their backsides. But in sophomore year,
my mind broke open like buds on a spring cherry tree. I didn't
"take" classes, I consumed them: anthropology, biology, cognitive
psychology, neurology, philosophy. After three years devouring the
undergraduate curriculum, I applied for a grant to an experimental
master's/doctoral program at Columbia. I was admitted. I knew my
parents wouldn't pay for such a "waste of time," so I got a job taking
care of the fifth graders no one else wanted to teach in a Harlem
elementary school to pay my tuition.

I didn't think teaching had anything to do with my Promise. I
just assumed it was a way of earning enough money to pursue the
questions that nagged me more than my mother. Why couldn't my
father learn to read when he was such a brilliant leader? Why was I
so miserable at learning to throw a softball or swim even though I
could master Latin with ease? The kids I was teaching were another
riddle. They came to school with rat bites on their cheeks, but my
grandmother had taught me that each one of them mattered to
the world in a very specific way. I assumed they were all riddles. I
noticed that Myron did best when he bounced a basketball while
saying the alphabet but spaced out when looking at written words
on a page. Jason hated phonics, but he could focus his eyes on a
whole paragraph, read it silently, and then draw what it was about.

Charlene could read only if she was in a rocking chair or pacing around the room.

None of the classes I was taking at Columbia helped me to understand these differences. I was taught how to classify, recognize, and treat *pathology*. This would have been useful if I wanted to help these kids get sick, go crazy, or grow up dumb, but never once did I ever hear a professor describe what a healthy human mind is, how it learns, or how one mind can communicate effectively with another.

Just as my grandmother had predicted, inspiring life-giving forces were also available to me. In the spring of my last year, I took a course at NYU with a brilliant neuroscientist named E. Roy John. He considered himself a quantitative electroencephalographist. Whatever that was, he reminded me most of a very tall dessert cactus, a night-blooming cereus, that produces immense white blossoms every June. In Roy's case, the blossoms opened when he placed little electrodes all over a person's skull and hooked them up to electroencephalographic equipment he had invented. I stood next to him and watched in awe as a child's brain lit up in its own unique way. He had developed a mechanism to actually watch a human think and learn! I knew that what I was seeing would change the way I thought and taught for the rest of my life.

One by one, I brought the kids from Harlem to the lab and we hooked each one up. I suggested specific things for them to think about. Myron's brain lit up when he imagined doing kinesthetic activities such as running. It spaced out, however, when he thought about writing or reading. Jason's brain lit up imagining writing or drawing but spaced out with auditory tasks such as speaking or music. Miranda's spaced out imagining running or dancing but lit up when she thought about talking or singing. Both Roy and I were stunned. Child after child gave us more corroboration that, although each brain's structure was similar, *each one was energized by a different method of processing information.*

One night, while listening to a concert of "Rhapsody in Blue" by George Gershwin, it dawned on me that brains functioned just like musical instruments. Instruments all used vibration to produce sounds, but some did it with wind, some with strings. You played some by bowing strings, others by strumming. What if all human brains produced "thought," but in different sequences or patterns of visual, auditory, and kinesthetic input to perform the act we call "thinking?" What if knowing which sequence a child innately used would help each of those "difficult, unteachable, disabled" kids in Harlem "play" the music we call learning?

This understanding was more of an uncovering than a discovering. It has continued to fascinate, obsess, and magnetize me for fifty-five years. But I also realized that making sure each child I came in contact with knew specifically how he or she mattered was even more important. I hung a sheet of newsprint for each child I taught on the battered walls of my Harlem classroom and put his or her name at the top. A half hour before the final bell rang each day, I asked them to stand in front of any paper and write one way that particular student had made their day better. By the time the bus arrived, each sheet of newsprint was full. At the end of the school year, I typed up the contents of each child's newsprint pages. I told them my grandmother's Promise story, and I then read each of their papers aloud to the whole class.

Three decades later, Charlene somehow found me. She wrote to say that she was the first in her family to graduate both high school and college. Hanging next to her diplomas, she had framed that paper reminding her of the Promise she carried in the world.

Blessed, Blissed, Pissed, Dissed

I was leading a retreat called "Time Out" at the Sundance Resort with my husband Andy, my son David, his wife Angie, and our colleague Mary Jane. We had no idea that in two days, the World Trade Center in New York City would be attacked. Most of the fifteen participants were senior leaders of a large tech company that had just been bought by an even larger tech firm. Although the men and women were only in their forties, the severance packages they had been offered were so large that they'd never need to work again. The question that dragged each of them to the Utah mountains was "Now What?"

I wasn't exactly sure how to begin the first session that morning, so I did what came naturally: I told a story: *Once upon a long time ago, in a place very far from here, there was a desperately poor village nestled at the base of the Himalayan mountains. In the center of town, there was a huge clay statue of the Buddha. No one knew who had built it or why. Every sunrise, the monks and villagers sat at its base to chant prayers. Then they went on with their daily chores. One day, while sweeping snow off the statue with a straw broom, a young monk noticed a small crack in the clay. He tried to ignore it, but as the sun rose, he could see something glinting from deep inside. Not knowing what to do, he ran to the cave of the head monk, telling him that the Buddha was broken and something shiny was within it. The head monk was dismissive, not even looking up from his papers. "That statue has been here for generations. There are many cracks in it. Leave me alone. I am very busy."*

The boy sheepishly went back to his sweeping. By now, the sun was higher in the sky. He couldn't keep himself from peeking into the crack one more time. Sure enough, there was something shining in there. Finally, he went to his mother, who trusted her son enough to follow him back to the statue. She saw the glinting too. She ran and gathered the other women. They all saw the shine. In less than ten minutes, everyone from the village was sitting around the statue trying to decide what to do. The head monk took a chisel and began to chip carefully around the crack. The glinting increased. Soon, no one could deny that under the outer layer of ordinary clay, there was a gold statue waiting to be revealed.

The townspeople argued late into the night. Should they destroy the clay Buddha and never have to worry again about money or leave it as it had always been? Finally, the head monk turned to the boy who had found the crack in the first place and asked him what he thought. Given this new recognition, the young boy was no longer afraid to speak. "I think the monks who built this Buddha must have known what they were doing. No one would want to steal or destroy an ordinary clay statue. But one made of precious gold would be the object of everyone's desire."

The monk nodded. Putting a hand on the boy's shoulder, he said, "Maybe each of us is meant to learn that, underneath our ordinary exterior, there is gold at our core."

At our retreat, Emily, a lanky blonde woman sitting across from me, raised her hand tentatively. "It's a quaint story, Dr. Markova, but what has it got to do with why we're here?" She chewed on her bottom lip before continuing. "I'm forty-five years old and have been quite successful as the first female CTO in the company. It wasn't easy, believe me. I was the only person in my family to go to college. I never took vacations, sick days, or even holidays. I've had to work harder than any man would to get where I am today. This retreat is a first for me. I don't have the slightest idea what my 'gold' is or how that's relevant to what I'm going to do with the rest of my life."

Her words were sharp, clipped, her voice threatening to detonate into shrapnel if she let it loose. Her right hand was clenched. I went over and sat next to her, looking down at the fist in her lap. Very slowly, I said, "The cells in my body understand completely what it takes to be the first woman in a leadership position. How challenging it must be to have to let go of that." I continued to stare at her hand. Emily looked down at the fist but didn't open her fingers. She just shrugged. I continued. "There is an old Japanese saying: 'Unclench the hand of thought.' For you and me to get where we are in life, Emily, we've had to grab every tiny opportunity. We've had to know the answer to every question we were asked. But what was the solution back then can now become the problem, especially when the question that is being put to us is, 'Now What?' "

Emily nodded, saying nothing, but her neck muscles softened and her eyes rimmed with tears. I extended my right hand clenched tightly into a fist in front of us and continued. "Nothing can get into a hand, or a mind, that is closed like this—not criticism, not insults, not put-downs. But it's also true that no ideas or insights can get in, either." As I spoke, she extended her arm like mine, fist facing upwards. I slowly opened my fingers. "What would it mean, what would it feel like, to 'open the hand of thought?' " Each of our fingers unfolded slowly like peony petals in the spring. I slid my open hand under hers and asked if she was open to wondering about two questions until the next session. She nodded immediately.

"The first question, Emily, is what have you ever done that makes you feel both blissed out and blessed?" I waited for a nod and then went on, "The second question is what makes you feel pissed because something or someone that you care about is being disrespected?"

Letting her arm sink slowly down to her side, Emily smiled. "OK. Blissed and blessed, pissed and dissed, right?"

I looked out at the rest of the group, who were also smiling. "Right. I'm suggesting that all of us spend the afternoon in solitude held in the bowl of these mountains, wondering about when in our lives do we feel blissed and blessed and when do we feel pissed and dissed."

After dinner, before we reconvened, Dave set up a video camera in the back of the room. Angie, who is a brilliant asker of open questions, sat next to Emily in the front. After the group gathered, the red light on the video began to blink. I asked everyone to "open the hand of thought" by observing without analyzing what was going to happen next. Angie leaned forward and asked Emily what she had discovered in solitude. The response was immediate. "The pissed and dissed were easy. They just popped into my mind while I was hiking. It pisses me off big time when girls and young women interested in science and math subjects are disrespected and redirected to more 'appropriate' majors. Furthermore, if they do manage to go on, they're not even considered for senior technical positions." Emily's cheeks were flushed. "In spite of that, I feel blessed to have had a remarkable mentor who is the CFO at our company headquarters. It's always felt as if she had my back. That's one of the hardest parts about having to leave the company."

Angie nodded and asked quietly, "What about the blissed?"

Emily shrugged. "I feel blissed when I walk in the country with my dog, but that doesn't really count."

Angie asked her about some of the places she had hiked. "When else do you feel blissed like that?" She leaned forward as if listening Emily into speech.

"Strange as it seems, I also used to feel blissed when I volunteered to help the kids at the homeless shelter near where I live do their math homework. I never thought of that as blissed until this moment, but it was just the same feeling as I have when hiking."

I nodded and asked Dave to replay the video of that conversation without sound. I invited the rest of the group to call out what they noticed. At first, we were all quiet, but, after a few minutes, people started to laugh. Mary Jane commented that it looked as if Emily lit up. A man next to me said that Emily had become completely energized and enlivened talking about the kids. Everyone else nodded in agreement. Dave replayed it one more time with the sound turned on. Sure enough, as soon as Emily started to talk about helping the kids, her back straightened, something akin to a grin crept across her face, and both hands conducted her words like musical notes. In short, she lit up.

We spent the rest of the evening with everyone in the group interviewing one another while Dave circulated with the video camera. People then got to see themselves answering the questions and discovering what made them light up.

As we were about to close the session, I wrote the following formula on the flip chart in the front of the room: P = pd+b+b-I, and then explained, "In Emily's honor I improvised this formula that I learned from author Timothy Gallwey. The big 'P' stands for the Promise Life made to the world the moment you were born. The little 'pd' stands for what makes you feel pissed off about the disrespect around you; 'b' is for the blessings in your life, and the second 'b' is for what you do that makes you feel blissed. Does anyone want to guess what the 'I' represents?"

Emily's open hand waved in the air and she immediately called out, "I read Galway too! 'I' is for interference! The external and internal ways all of that potential gets interfered with."

I reached out, opening my palm to slap hers, and said, "What I realized when I walked in solitude this afternoon is that telling the stories that have yeasted me and braiding them together so I can help others realize their potential fulfills the Promise of my life. Like you, I've interfered with it by closing my mind to the possibility that it could be relevant or useful. Many thanks for the lesson, Emily!"

In two days' time, the World Trade Center was destroyed, and each of us realized just how relevant our learning could be.

How Do I Call When I Want the Promise to Answer?

I am in trouble at school again. The teacher tells my mother that I keep staring out the window and won't pay attention. I have no idea what she's talking about. Daddy pays tolls when he crosses the George Washington Bridge, but I've never seen anyone paying attention. To tell the truth, I don't even really know what attention is, but everyone wants some from me. As I click the front door to her apartment shut behind me, I decide to ask Grandma. She's standing in front of the old oak bureau in her bedroom. While I tell her about what the teacher said, she brushes her hair. It's like a dense cloud of white silk and has never been cut in her entire life.

The only thing on top of the bureau is a small carved camphorwood box. She places her brush down next to the silver hand mirror my father gave her and puts the box in her palm, saying, "Your mind, like this box, can both open and close. Your attention makes both possible."

She stretches the box out to me, and I pry the lid open very carefully with my thumbnail. Inside, there is a musty smell and a handful of dirt.

"Where does it come from, Grandma?"

"Home."

I look around the apartment, but she shakes her head. Then I figure out that she must mean Russia, the old country. "What's it for?"

She takes a pinch of the dirt between her fingers and sifts it back
into the box. Her voice gets cobwebby as she answers, "When
Grandpa and I fled from the old country, I had to leave so much
behind, even my first two children and my brother. So I put a
handful of home inside this little box to carry with me. We were on
a boat crossing the ocean for so very long, but when we finally got
off and I stepped onto Ellis Island, the first thing I did was to put
a pinch of that dirt down beneath my feet. That made the foreign
ground home. I had never seen an ocean before I got on that boat."
She wrapped her thin arms around me and rocked back and forth
as she continued, "It was so wide and so deep, Ketzaleh. Who could
imagine such a thing existed beyond the potato fields? I watched
it day after day. Once, I even tasted it on my tongue. It was salty
just like tears. Finally I decided that a person's mind is just like that
ocean. Some thoughts float and splash like waves on the surface,
some things sink and go all the way down, deep, deep, down to the
very bottom."

"But Grandma, if something falls into the ocean and sinks down
that far, can you ever find it?"

Her explanation comes very slowly. "That's what your attention is
for, Ketzaleh. Thoughts can splash noisily here and there on the top,
pulled by whatever grabs them. But if you just let them sink down
a little way, they float around. People call that daydreaming. At the
very bottom of your mind, your attention is wide and silent."

"Grandma, that's just what happens to me in school when I stare
out the window instead of practicing my multiplication tables! But
why does my teacher say attention is something you have to pay,
like when you cross the George Washington Bridge?"

She holds my hand ever so gently and leads me into the kitchen, where she fills up the big glass bread bowl with water. "Attention is the simplest kind of love, my darling. Maybe your teacher has forgotten how to float down into the heart of her own mind. A lot of grown-ups do. Maybe she's afraid she'll drown in all the feelings she's dropped down there. I don't know why people say you have to 'pay,' Ketzaleh. Maybe it's because as your attention takes you down, down, down, it's like crossing a bridge into a different world."

"But what happens at the bottom of the ocean of your mind? What's down there?"

"Oh, my darling, there are things called memories and feelings and possibilities and dreams and ideas, and even stories. Everything you've ever learned is down there, even if you don't remember it when you are splashing up on the surface. And guess what? You can find the Promise down there. Some people call it your soul or spirit or wisdom. To me, it's the Promise."

Looking into her eyes, I can see it all in the ocean of my mind.

"And your attention will make your thinking very different down there. You don't have to hold on to anything. You float around, and your mind opens to the whole, wide floor where everything falls eventually. The waves of thinking splash above you, but it is totally silent down there."

I actually feel as if I'm floating while I watch her open the camphorwood box and listen to her whisper, "Boxes, hearts, and minds can be opened or closed. They're capable of both, yes?" It takes me a moment to think about what she's just said. "Let your attention open as wide as a wing. You may hear songs or see

swimmy pictures or get ideas down there. Maybe you'll come back
up with an answer to a question you've been wondering about for
a long time, or maybe a bigger way of knowing something will just
pop up on the surface with you. Maybe you'll just feel easier with a
question that's been bothering you."

"Grandma, is that how you got so wise even though you never went
to school or had teachers saying mean things about you?"

Her eyes sparkle stars at me and she kisses my forehead without
saying a word. It doesn't matter, though, because I don't need to
ask any more questions. In some way beyond words, I understand
exactly what she means.

Argue for Limitations and They're Mine

I was barely nineteen when I first met the pioneering
hypnotherapist Milton Erickson. I was still a graduate student in
New York City, and he had been invited by the school's clinical
supervisors to give us a lecture on medical hypnosis. I discovered,
reading whatever I could about him, that he'd had polio twice and,
as a result, had to use canes to get around. He was also completely
tone-deaf and color-blind (with the exception of purple).
Nonetheless, he considered every constraint to be an opportunity
within which he could create a new possibility. When he went
to a concert, for example, he rolled his wheelchair to the front of
the theater, then turned it to face the audience and watched them
throughout the performance. After the applause settled down, he
told his wife Betty which instruments were off-key. He discovered
simply by observing the reactions of the people.

Before the lecture, the clinical supervisors had written down a
random number on a piece of paper. Each seat in the amphitheater
had a small brass plate on it with an etched number. Their challenge
to Dr. Erickson was to hypnotize whoever sat down in the seat
with that number while simultaneously delivering his lecture
on hypnosis. Up until that moment, I'd never won any kind of a
contest in my life.

When Dr. Erickson had finished speaking, I noticed that everyone
else stood up to leave, but I just sat there, my right arm floating in
front of my face, my legs completely uninterested in moving. He
approached me slowly, red rubber cane tips squeaking on the dark
oak floor. Leaning over me, he said in a gravelly whisper, "There is
a part of your mind, the unconscious mind, that knows everything
you most need to know, even when you don't know that you know

it…and you can trust that part of your mind, trust it deeply." After I left the amphitheater, I felt free in the same way I used to when leaving Grandma's apartment.

I studied Milton's work for decades after that day, not because I wanted to learn hypnosis, but because I wanted to understand how I could widen my attention and notice where I was already free. I learned more from him than from all the clinical supervisors in graduate school combined, who kept insisting I should constantly notice and classify everything that was wrong with every person I worked with, label it, and record the pathology on a standardized form. Dr. Erickson taught me one thing that was more important than anything else I learned in graduate school: he taught me that my role was to help as many powerful minds as I could to grow by focusing on what was right about what appeared to be wrong with someone. With him, I discovered that having an asset-focus— exploring a person's history of health and sanity—was an important step to living a life I could love.

Milton's teachings did more for me than I ever can say. My only regret was that I never hugged him. Hugging wasn't "the thing" back then that it is now. Besides, I had no idea how you hug someone who uses canes or is in a wheelchair. Nonetheless, I always wanted to hug him. One day, decades after that first lecture, I was visiting his home office in Phoenix for what turned out to be the last time I would ever see him. More than anything, I wanted to tell him how much I appreciated what his teachings had done for me. More than anything, I wanted to hug him just once. At the end of our time together, I gathered up my belongings and haltingly walked past his desk. My fingers reached out to briefly touch the purple telephone sitting on it as I moved toward the sliding glass door where I was to exit. I hesitated while turning to face him, knowing it was the last time I'd have a chance to hug him. But all I could allow myself to do was mumble, "Thank you very much, Dr. Erickson." I walked out slowly and slid the door closed behind me.

As I took a step away from the house, I noticed he had wheeled over to that door. Sliding it open, he called me in that gravelly one-of-a-kind voice of his and said, "Dawna…" I stopped in my tracks, sure he was going to reach out and hug me. Instead, slowly, oh so slowly, he slid the door closed and as he did so, said, "Never create limitations…where…there are no limitations given!"

I heard a click as he locked the door and wheeled away.

In Pursuit of the Dangerously Possible

Each time I think I have learned to open my mind and widen my attention, Life gives me another opportunity to practice thinking beyond the habitual limitations I create for myself. On the day of this story, I was standing next to two people who I assumed were father and daughter. Antonio's hair was silver, his olive skin tanned and weathered with creases in the corners of his amber eyes. The word "elegant" came to mind immediately, though I can't say why. Carolina was almost impossibly beautiful, with high cheekbones, flawless skin, and gleaming chestnut hair. As she moved across the veranda, her hands gestured toward the leather couch, inviting me to sit. She was lithe, sleek, as green-eyed as a jungle cat.

She had called me two weeks before in the dead of a stormy Vermont night after reading one of my books. She told me I was their last hope. There was something in her voice, though, that made me want to agree with whatever she asked. Carolina told me she was calling to invite Andy and I to meet with her and her husband Antonio and their family at their Caribbean home over Christmas vacation. She explained that they all needed to discuss a "leetle" family problem they were having. The thought of a tropical two weeks, as well as Carolina's seductive voice, was enticing, but I was well aware that being someone's "last hope" was a sure setup to prove that a situation is truly hopeless. Nonetheless, the prospect of working on a sultry island instead of spending the holidays in a blizzard provoked a "yes" from me before reason could take over.

A few days before Christmas, the four of us sat literally in the lap of tropical luxury. The price of the leather couch was more than our monthly mortgage payment. Carolina explained that their marriage a year earlier had caused an immense rift in Antonio's family.

They'd consulted with a priest and then a mediator before calling us. Carolina explained that when she and Antonio first met, he was teaching a seminar about leadership at the college where she was then still a student. Cutting to the chase, Antonio crossed his long legs and explained that at the time, his then-wife had been dying of cancer. Marlena, his oldest daughter, hadn't spoken to Carolina since the wedding. Sophia, the younger of the two, also refused to connect with her new stepmother. Antonio's right eyebrow rose slightly and his lips thinned as he explained that he had brought the whole family together for this two-week vacation in the hope of repairing the rupture between them. Any time the whole family gathered, it was excruciatingly uncomfortable. Carolina told us that there were several houses on the property. Marlena and Sophia stayed down the road with their children and husbands. The sons-in-law and grandchildren didn't know what to do. No one knew what to do.

Early the next morning, Andy went for a walk on the beach with Sophia. I invited Marlena to go with me. She was as long-legged as her father and was impeccably dressed in a light blue silk blouse, linen slacks, and large gold shell earrings. She seemed to be standing still even when strolling. The tide was coming in, leaving the deserted narrow beach littered with plastic soda bottles and tangled fishing line. She kept bending over to pick up the debris, reminding me for some reason of a wounded flamingo. In a smooth voice with a glassy surface, Marlena explained that she had been coming to that beach since she was a little girl and the plastic garbage that floated in every morning broke her heart.

I widened my attention by listening to the surf on the shore and watching white egrets fly over our heads. After several minutes, I told her that Andy and I were there because her father's heart was also breaking, but for a different reason. Her jaw clamped tight

like the fishing wire she was trying to untangle. She snarled that
Carolina was young enough to be her own daughter.

I asked if she had been very close to her mother. After a long pause,
Marlena gazed at the horizon and explained that she had been
with her mother in the hospital when she died. "I was with Madre
every minute. She knew about Carolina, of course, and made me
promise that I would never speak to her, never. I intend to keep that
promise." There was a simmering threat that seemed to live behind
her eyes as she looked at me and then turned her back, dumping
the garbage into a large barrel. What was truly stuck in the family
became obvious to me in that moment.

After conferring with Andy, we decided to meet with the whole
family on the beach that afternoon. Fourteen of them stood with
the two of us in a circle, eight grandchildren and two sons-in-law
included. There was a huge mound of plastic in the center—bottles,
fishing line, palm fronds, coconuts, and other debris that Andy had
gathered on his walk with Sophia that morning. I explained that
their collective task was to create a sculpture of the family using
that debris. They had forty-five minutes to finish and must do it in
complete silence. I suggested that they should somehow include the
family's history, present state, and best possible future. There were
a few giggles, but the kids led the way and everyone else followed.
As they worked, all I could hear was the sound of the surf and the
seagulls flying in circles above us.

An hour later, we all walked slowly and silently around the six-foot
high creation, which seemed to be a living sea creature. I slowly
called out questions, asking that they not answer, but instead just
"read" the statue and wonder. "What's its name? What does it make
you feel like inside? What is most beautiful about it? What was
your part in creating it? What does it have to teach you about how

to grow a successful future together? What did you learn that you could do to make that happen?"

Then I asked that one by one, they go around the circle and respond to these questions. Angelina, the littlest, shouted, "I think its name is GBL for Great, Big, Love. I learned that big people can be fun to play with even when they're not talking to each other." Paulo, her older brother, went next and said, "Yeah, nobody bossed us. Nobody got mad. We all made something together that's so cool and that none of us could do alone." The intimacy of the moment was palpable.

When they were finished, I asked the kids to create a landscape for the statue and photograph it while the adults went back to the veranda to talk about how they could make it come alive. As we settled in, Carolina had tears on her face. Looking at us, she said, "The word for problem in Spanish is 'problema,' and the word for solution is 'solucion.' Just now on the beach, we all were part of a problem becoming a solution, and nobody had to say a word to make that happen. Maybe together what we all created can help the problem in this family somehow become a solution. I don't know how. Maybe no one does. But together I pray that we can figure it out."

All eyes darted immediately to Marlena. She bit her lip. Antonio interrupted and said, " 'Problema' sounds like a feminine word, but it is in fact masculine. I realize now that I, the man of the family, caused the problem between all of us."

Marlena looked around the circle and then ran her fingers through her hair before saying, "Well, that may be true, but I know that the women here can be the solution, and I want to be part of it.

I don't know how, without betraying my mother's dying wish, but perhaps…"

Sophia leaned over and embraced her sister, whispering quietly, "I heard somewhere that when you cast someone out of your heart, it makes it shrink, and your whole world gets smaller. When we were creating the statue, you were the one who made a big heart in the middle with squished soda cans. Perhaps we can find a way to grow our women's hearts big enough so we can somehow connect with the other woman in this family."

I looked at the two of them, feeling something invisible drop and settle in the group. Andy leaned over and put his big, warm hand on Antonio's shoulder, saying, "What was dead debris is now a Great, Big, Alive creation. Perhaps the promise and curse that got you all stuck can now, with the family's support and creativity, be freed to become a blessing."

Later that evening, sitting next to the fireplace in the living room, Antonio and I debriefed about what had happened earlier, while Andy did the same in the dining room with the sisters and their families. "At first, I couldn't figure out what in the world we were going to do with all that plastic garbage," admitted Antonio. "It's been the bane of my existence for several years: junk floating in the tide each morning. We haven't been able to get rid of it, and now you were asking us to play with it. I thought you were loco, and so was I for asking you to come here!" He smiled softly. "But nothing else had worked with Carolina and my daughters, so I decided to give my 'permiso'—a masculine word, by the way." He winked at me.

I explained that sometimes the most effective way to work with being stuck is to externalize it, to put it out there at arm's length

so you can widen your attention and notice where you are free.
"To tell you the truth, when we first arrived, I had no idea what we
were going to do. Marlena could not possibly break that promise
she made to her mother on her deathbed. And she may continue
to need to honor it, even now." I leaned back into the down-filled
cushions on the couch. "I decided not to hold the same limitations
in my own mind that you all had in yours. That enabled me to think
freely enough to notice what we could create within the constraints
that we couldn't change."

Antonio told me that he had grown up as the only son of a rich
family. At sixteen, he took a job as a deckhand on a sailboat. He
learned how to look out at the stars on the horizon and just let
his mind go wide so he could imagine the kind of future he really
wanted. "Being able to play together today as a family and then step
back and see the possibility we created from a pile of garbage made
it possible for my mind to go wide again. At the very least, we now
all have a magnetic north now so we can honor the true richness of
what our family was and also reach for the true wealth of what we
can become."

Taking my right hand in his, Antonio kissed the back of it and said,
"I am deeply grateful for you and your husband helping us discover
how we can live a life we can love together, Dawna." Then he looked
up, winked, and said, "By the way, 'gratitude' is a feminine word."

How Do I Notice Where I'm Already Free?

Late one rainy Friday afternoon, Grandma and I are making what she calls "Angry Cookies." I had arrived that morning scowling only to collapse in the safety of her lap. My parents had been fighting with each other, flinging loud curses back and forth across our living room like tennis balls that bounced against my heart. I kept trying to catch each one, but I didn't know how. I hated it. I was only a little kid, after all.

After absorbing my tears in her apron, Grandma reaches up into the cupboard and pulls down a big glass jar of oatmeal and another of pure white sugar. Then she opens the icebox and takes out a dish of bright yellow butter. After measuring some of each into a huge glass bowl, she holds out a wooden spoon to me. I step up and begin to mix the batter.

"Grandma, why do you call them Angry Cookies?"

"You'll find out, my darling."

I stir and chop, but the dough is so stiff I can't get it to blend together. I put the spoon down and try to work it with the fingers of my right hand, but they just keep getting stuck in the thick glop. The more I try, the more entangled my fingers become.

"Ketzaleh, you're putting all of your attention where you're stuck. But that's only a very small part of you. Notice the rest instead. Notice you can breathe and lift your feet. Notice you have another hand. Notice where you are free."

I take a deep breath and jiggle my toes in my black patent leather shoes. Then, aha! I notice the sink is within reach of my free left hand. I turn the faucet on, stretch over to it, and run my fingers under the water until they're slippery wet. I put that hand in the bowl with my stuck right one. Sure enough, the dough gets squishy, and my other fingers are now free also. At that moment, Grandma says, "Just so! Now take each tennis ball curse you heard from your parents and make a nice round cookie out of it."

My fingers know exactly how to do this. Each shout in my head becomes a perfectly round ball. Grandma places her fingertip on top of one ball and flattens it into a perfect cookie.

"Your turn, Ketzaleh. Press the promise print at the end of your finger into each cookie."

As I press down on the dough, questions begin to float in my mind like wispy clouds after a storm. If my parents love me so much, why do they curse at each other? If there are no more Cossacks or concentration camps, why aren't they happy all the time? I tell Grandma what I'm thinking.

She brushes strands of curly red hair off my forehead and whispers, "You ask such wonderful questions when you notice where you're free. Maybe it would be good to ask them of your Mommy and Daddy so they can get unstuck, too, and find the answers." Grandma's dark eyes light up like stars in a night sky. "All you have to remember is that some questions and some stories can open people's minds so they can notice where they are already free."

"But Grandma, what if it's someone I don't love or don't really know?"

"Ketzaleh, Ketzaleh. Love is a choice you make, just like noticing where you are free instead of where you are stuck."

I kind of understand what she's telling me, and I know it must have something to do with my Promise, but it's all still sticky to me. "Grandma, does this have to do with what you taught me about wondering and telling stories?"

As she places each cookie carefully on the metal pan, she explains slowly, "Just so, Ketzaleh. You can choose to wonder about people you meet instead of thinking you know what's wrong with them and why they're stuck. Just listen to the stories they tell themselves. Then hold them in the warmth of your heart wondering where and how they're already free. This will help both your heart and theirs spread bigger and wider."

"Like the cookies will in the oven!"

She lets me place the last Angry Cookie on the tray and slide it into the oven. "If you curse someone to try to put them out of your mind, Ketzaleh, it makes your heart shrink. If instead, you hold them there and just wonder, you might find a question or a story rising up that will help you both get free."

"So my Promise of wondering wide and telling stories is like the cookies, Grandma? It can help us grow wider instead of being stuck and grow bigger than what we're afraid of. I can smell it happening in that oven now. That's a pretty delicious Promise, Grandma!"

A Body of Wisdom

When I was eight years old, Dr. Morris Rossenbrach told my
mother that I was "constitutionally inadequate." Mind you, I was
sitting on a turquoise blue plastic chair right next to them, hearing
every word. When she asked him what that meant, he said that my
physical structure was not adequate to do what it was supposed to
do. This basic message was subsequently confirmed by physical
education teachers, camp counselors, my father's beatings with
a belt (which were of course "for my own good"), adolescent boy
friends who shamed me for being flat-chested, and the man who
raped me when I was fifteen years old.

Everything I'd learned from my grandmother was locked in a safe-
deposit box that I kept in my heart when she died and I entered
puberty. I stepped over an invisible threshold into the enchantment
of the story my parents dressed me in: I was a Perfect Princess,
and all my promises would be realized when I found the Prince. At
twenty-one, I met a man who looked like the Prince was supposed
to look and was even the perfect religion. He gave me a nearly
perfect two-carat diamond ring. My parents dug deep into their
savings to pay for a nearly perfect wedding at the Hampshire House
Hotel on Central Park Avenue. The night before the ceremony,
however, I did a very not-perfect thing while they were sound
asleep: grabbing a large pair of scissors I found on the desk, I
chopped off as much of my knee-length curly red hair as I could
and flushed it down the toilet, one handful after another. The next
morning, my hysterical mother took me to the beauty salon in the
lobby, where what remained of my hair was styled and sprayed
stiffly into a very short, stylishly perfect bubble cut.

But bubbles pop. My illusions about the Prince did in no time. Dr. Samuel Freudenberger, my new husband's psychiatrist, insisted that I was a frigid castrating female. I did my best to become who he wanted me to be and to get pregnant as quickly as possible, whether I enjoyed doing so or not. My body wouldn't cooperate. After three miscarriages, Dr. Freudenberger shrugged and agreed that I was just constitutionally inadequate. A few weeks later, I dreamt that a white-winged falcon emerged from dark clouds and circled over me. In it, I was rocking a bassinet covered in white batiste threaded with pale blue silk ribbons. The next morning, I discovered I was again pregnant. In the months that followed, my body did everything it was supposed to do and did it all perfectly.

I went into labor on the day predicted. The diagnoses of Doctors Rossenbrach and Freudenberger, who had never conceived or carried a baby, were replaced by the wisdom and guidance of my midwife grandmother. Years before I could understand, she had told me that I would someday have a very easy "walking labor." My body followed her prediction perfectly. As the due date approached, I walked around cleaning the refrigerator, feeding the cat, and ironing underwear while feeling nothing more serious than menstrual cramps. By the time my water broke and I reached Mt. Sinai Hospital, I was already seven centimeters dilated. The Prince dropped me off at the Emergency entrance and returned to the car to smoke a joint and hang out for the duration.

I had chosen Dr. Weinstein because he had exactly the same deep greeny eyes that my grandmother did. He examined me and called for a gurney, shouting "Stat!" Someone wearing a blue paper suit propelled me to the delivery room. The double doors exploded open. Someone told me to pant until Dr. Weinstein was finished scrubbing up. I ignored all instructions except those of my grandma and my own body's urge to squat. Dr. Weinstein rushed in and tried to persuade me to slow down. "Lie down Dawna. Not so fast, not so fast!" People had been telling me that my whole life. But I wasn't following the good doctor. I was panting and squatting the way my grandmother taught all the women she midwifed.

At first, my mind told me that I was constitutionally inadequate and I just wasn't up to the task. I'd better get the hell out of that hospital. I shouted at Dr. Weinstein that I wasn't strong enough to do it. He tried to reassure me. I screamed, "Well, then *you* do it!" Who did he and all those blue-papered people think they were? They didn't even know me. I was all alone in a frigid body and I wanted to get the hell out of there. My body told me that was not an option. I looked up into the blinding glass eye over the table, remembered the white-winged falcon dream, and surrendered. I heard my grandmother's papery soft voice saying, "They all told you it would be too painful, too difficult, and that you wouldn't be strong enough. What do they know! Don't believe them. It's just hard work, like digging dirt or pushing a piano uphill. And you can do it, because you're not alone. Millions of women throughout time have done this and are doing it at this very minute. They'll help you. Imagine them behind you, next to you, surrounding you, telling you that your body knows what to do. Breathe and push. Trust them. Trust your body."

I could feel all those women circling, the ones who had given birth and the ones who at that very moment were also giving birth someplace on the earth. They circled me, lifted me, reached out to me with hidden hands. They inspired the baby through the doorway of my body into that glorious moment. As I watched David's head crown, I laughed in a way I never had before. No matter how much work I had been doing, I knew I wanted to welcome my son with laughter. Life was making a new Promise to the world, and I was helping midwife it.

Dr. Weinstein's voice came to me, full of delight. "It's over now, Dawna. Your son is born, and he is perfect."

My son? In that buoyant moment when the miraculous lump of life was in my arms, I knew that Dr. Rossenbrach and Dr. Freudenberger were wrong. And I knew that Dr. Weinstein was wrong, too. This jewel of Life was not my son, but a miracle entire unto himself. And as I witnessed his unfurling, I also realized that my body was enough. We were all threads in the amazing web of promises Life made to the world.

A nurse approached me with an injection to dry up my milk, explaining that it was best to get the baby used to formula immediately. I just laughed and placed David on my formerly flat chest. My breasts were now filling up and spilling over. No one else in the maternity wing of Mount Sinai was nursing, but that no longer mattered to me. I rocked and hummed the lullabies my grandmother used to sing to me. And as a river of milk flowed through me, I told David stories about the Promise he carried in every cell of his body and how it would inspire him to risk growing the gift that only he could bring to the world.

May It Be So

I was standing in front of a thousand school administrators and
teachers in the grand ballroom of a hotel in Miami, Florida, about
to give a keynote speech entitled, "Every Child Carries a Promise."
A week before, there had been a shooting in Parkland and seventeen
students had been killed. In spite of my carefully typed notes on the
podium, all I could think about was Jerome. That was the only place
I could begin.

*I met Jerome in a broom closet, which had been assigned to me as
my "office." He was in the sixth grade and lived in a migrant labor
camp in Coconut Creek with his aunt and two sisters. I was the
school "Learning Specialist," and he had been referred to me because
he could not read. The principal, Eloise Barney, told me he had
been classified as trainably retarded; he was incapable of learning
therefore, and my job was to keep him out of everyone else's way.*

*He was a big kid, even for fourteen, and had both mischief and misery
shining from his wide brown eyes. Daily, he was sent to Eloise's office,
where she applied a large wooden paddle called the Convincer to his
backside and then sent him over to my office. Jerome wrapped his
bulging forearms across his rigid chest and declared, "You ain't gonna
make me learn to read." That made it unanimous. And a challenge. I
do love challenges.*

*Some of the other kids had told me that Jerome was the chess
champion of the labor camp. I found that curious. How could he
play chess so well if he was stupid? I went to watch him compete one
evening. No white teacher had ever set foot in that camp. I found
Jerome pacing in front of a chessboard set up on an old orange
crate. A large crowd of children and adults surrounded him. An old*

man sitting on the other side of the board moved a bishop. Jerome's
eyes got wide as he paced back and forth. Everyone was silent. Two
long strides brought him back to the board. Eyes narrowed, Jerome
pounced, moving a knight as he declared, "Checkmate!" The crowd
went wild, but he just smiled quietly and strolled away.

The next morning, when he entered the broom closet, I placed a
thick book on the upturned mop bucket that served as my desk.
It was covered in red leather, and the title was stamped in gold
letters: A History of the African American. Then I excused myself
for a few minutes and left him alone. When I returned, Jerome was
thumbing through the pages; his eyes lit up as his fingers traced
over the photographs. He slammed it closed and demanded of me,
"How'd they get those folks all ironed flat like dat so they could fit in
the book?" The gold letters must have lured Jerome to look through
the pages, but it took me a minute to realize that he had never seen
photographs of black people in a book. I explained. He responded by
insisting, "You ain't gonna make me read that. You read it to me,
Missus Teacher."

I removed the book and replaced it with a chessboard and pieces,
offering him my terms: I would play one game of chess with him. If
he won, I'd read him the book. If I won, I'd teach him how to read
it for himself, no matter how long it took. The outcome was divine
intervention. I had only played chess a few times in my life, and
Jerome was definitely an expert, but I did win that game. And Jerome
did learn to read that book.

I recalled all I had discovered in graduate school about how different
brains process information differently. I asked Jerome dozens of
questions about how he had learned to play chess, knowing that there
would be a clue someplace as to how exactly he could learn to read. "I
gotta be standing up and moving around. And it's gotta be real quiet,

or I can't think. Then I make my eyes look at the board. When I close
them, I can see the whole thing in my mind. If it's quiet enough, I
hear a voice inside my head telling me which piece to move, and then
I see my hand doing it."

That was the secret formula I had been searching for. Phonics were
out. To teach him to read, I needed to follow the same pattern he used
to play chess. While he was pacing around, I traced words on his back
while he traced them in the air and saw them in his mind. Then he
said them to himself while looking at the book. It was laborious at
first, but he understood immediately what I was doing and joined in
figuring out how to apply that which he could do well to that which
he could not do at all. He began to read whole pages to himself with
100 percent comprehension. I learned as much as he did.

Several months later, after he had read the last page, I gave him the
book as a trophy. The next morning, however, I found it back on the
bucket. I raced over to the camp, but he was nowhere to be found. His
sister told me that it was time for them to move on to another camp.
He couldn't keep the book because he was afraid such a valuable
possession would get stolen. That would have hurt him too much. She
offered me a brown piece of paper torn from a shopping bag. On it,
Jerome had written:

> I don't know how to show
> the goodness of feeling
> right about what was wrong
> or so they said
> about my head.

> Thanks.

RISING   61

I looked out at the audience and spoke directly to them. "The statistical chance of Jerome being alive today is very slight. As you must know, African American men are an endangered species. Five years after Jerome learned to read that book, I left education permanently. I could no longer survive there. It was as if I had been trying to teach deep breathing in an oven with the gas turned on. Since then, I've been training parents, counselors, social workers, business leaders, and psychotherapists how to discover the unique way each child learns, so he or she can recognize their capacity to live a meaningful life. Most people tell me it's too much trouble with so many kids in a classroom and so much standardization demanded of them."

I paused long enough to feel my feet on the ground. "I decided to come here today so I could share what I learned from Jerome in a school only a few miles from the one where those seventeen young people were recently shot. I want you to understand that different children learn in different ways. It is our job to discover what the promise is within each of them and how to access it. Maybe one of you will have the chance to work with a sister, a cousin, or a brother of Jerome. That would make the circle complete. For now, I'd like to share a brief practice that will bless the future of the children who are already within your arms' reach." I asked how many knew five ways to curse a child who did something really annoying, frustrating, or even infuriating. Everyone laughed nervously and raised his or her hand. The administrator who had hired me was sitting in the front row, beginning to look very uncomfortable. He had no idea where I was going with this. Ignoring him, I asked how many knew five ways to bless the future of that child. A few hands were tentatively raised.

"I'd like to ask you to bring a child to mind who has been infuriating to you. For a moment or two, just wonder what the learning pattern

could be for something that child knows how to do well, a talent
perhaps. For one minute, wonder about how that pattern might be
used to transform the cursed behavior into something meaningful.
If you can't even imagine it, it won't be possible to help create
it, right? You can at least imagine them thriving, blossoming,
in a simple and real way. I invite you to finish this daydream by
whispering in your own mind, 'May it be so.' "

The room got so still I could hear my own breath. After a few
minutes, I asked how the experience had affected them. One person
called out "I feel energized." Another shouted, "I feel relaxed,
connected." Finally, the administrator in the front row yelled, "I feel
possible!" The woman sitting next to him said, "I want to bless the
future of all of the kids in Parkland." The silence in the room grew
thick again, rich as velvet. Then she called out, "May it be so!" One
by one, other voices from the back and the front and even from the
very edges of the room joined in. "May it be so!"

I asked people to notice what it felt like to be in a room where
the future of children who had previously been cursed was now
being blessed. I suggested that we call out the name of someone we
cared about who was not in the room, someone we would like to
experience the energy of a thousand people blessing. I heard names
of children, relatives, politicians, and others who were no longer
alive reverberating from the ballroom's white walls. I called out my
son David's name, my grandmother's, and then finally Jerome's.
Everyone in the room called out in unison, "May it be so."

Kneading

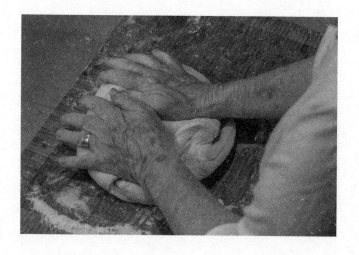

"

"...I think we are well-advised to keep on nodding terms with the people we used to be, whether we find them attractive company or not. Otherwise they turn up unannounced and surprise us, come hammering on the mind's door at 4 a.m. of a bad night, and demand to know who deserted them, who betrayed them, who is going to make amends. We forget all too soon the things we thought we could never forget. We forget the loves and the betrayals alike, forget what we whispered and what we screamed, forget who we were."

—**Joan Didion**

How Can I Never Lose Who I Really Am?

I seem to get lost a lot. It's my sister's fault. At least that's what my mother says. When I was just three months old, my sister took me for a walk in a large black baby carriage, which she left on the yellow painted lines in the middle of Ditmus Avenue in Brooklyn. It took the police several hours to find me. Supposedly, I wasn't even crying at the time.

I also seem to break bones a lot. Leg bones, arm bones, collarbones, funny bones: I've broken them all. My sister says it's because I was born a klutz. When I broke the bone in my right leg, she drew an ugly face on the cast. So it has taken a long time to climb the stairs to Grandma's today. I am carrying my favorite book, *The Wizard of Oz*, in a backpack so I can manage the crutches. The heroine, Dorothy, gets lost a lot, just like I do. I take the book under the kitchen table, where the red oilcloth cover hangs down and makes a tent I can hide under. Grandma comes in to check on the yeasting Sabbath bread, and I begin immediately to pelt her with the question that keeps rising in my mind.

"Grandma, why do I keep getting lost all the time? How will I ever find the Promise if I keep losing my way?"

She pulls me up onto her bony lap, cast and all, and puts her warm hand on top of mine. The veins on the back pop out like little rivers. Her skin has brown spots and is thin as onion skin. She moves our hands around and around. Each time they trace a bigger and bigger circle in the air. Then I recognize the shape.

"I know what that's called, Grandma! I just learned about it in school. It's a spiral."

Her eyes get crinkly in the corners. "*I* call it the Wisdom Trail."
She kisses the back of my neck where she says it tastes the sweetest,
saying, "In school, they teach you many things that you're supposed
to master, like reading and arithmetic. I don't know anything about
them, but I do know about things that are a mystery: bringing
babies into the world and discovering the Promise in people."

Ah, this is what I really want to hear about. Maybe the Wisdom
Trail is like the Yellow Brick Road. "Tell me about that, Grandma.
Will it keep me from getting lost?"

She keeps our hands moving in a spiral, up, around, out. "Well,
let's talk about that. You'll live many moments, Ketzaleh. If you
memorize them and the people that you love, they'll be planted on
the Island that is deep within your heart. When your body dies, that
Island goes with you."

"But Grandma, what if I rush and forget to memorize them. It's
hard to memorize my multiplication tables. Moments? People? I
don't know if I can do that. I'll get lost even more than I do now!"

Her eyes light up. "It's not as hard as you think, my darling. What's
most important is not to rush. You see, there is One who lives on
that Island who is always listening to your thoughts. Can you find
that One now?"

I think to myself that I won't be able to find that One, but then I
notice the one who is thinking that thought. I try not to bounce on
my Grandma's knees because I might hurt her, but I jiggle excitedly.
"Yes, Grandma. It's easy. There has to be one who is listening to my
thoughts, 'cause otherwise who would notice them?"

"Just so, Ketzaleh. That is the One who lives on the Island of your Heart. It has always been there and will always be there. And the more moments you love, the more will be planted on that Island. If a person rushes around and doesn't notice any moments, their Island will be like a desert because nothing will take root."

"And when I die, will that Island and the One Who Knows go with me?"

Without hesitation, she strokes the hair out of my eyes and nods. "You can learn to make the kind of choices that help you memorize your moments, Ketzaleh. You move through your moments making choices. Some will make you feel more alive, some will make you feel less. This is as it meant to be. Instead of marching ahead in a straight line, your life is meant to go like a spiral. Each time you make a choice that helps you love that moment, the spiral gets wider and wider and you get wiser and wiser."

I like the idea of a spiral path instead of a straight line. I especially like that I can't get lost on it. But I'm still confused. "OK, I get that, but how do I love a moment?"

As she answers, she takes a pencil and draws a little heart around the ugly face on my cast. "First you have to know how to make choices as you walk on the Wisdom Trail, Ketzaleh. You may choose to leap with one foot because it seems like it will be fun and it seems like it could grow the life in you. Let's call that your foot of risk. Then you may choose to feel safe and secure, so you root down right where you are with your other foot. You keep going back and forth: risk, safe, risk, safe, back and forth, back and forth. Understanding that will help you love your life."

I grin. Grandma must know I broke my leg bone by jumping off the merry-go-round at the park. Mommy said Joan should have been watching me better and I should stop being so wild and taking so many risks.

"Sometimes, Ketzaleh, people only make choices to stay safe. Then they get stuck and rigid, trying to control things all the time. The life force in them becomes more and more numb and dead, like yeast that doesn't rise."

Ah, that's my sister. She always chooses to make everything be just the same as it always has been. "But what about someone who only chooses to leap and take risks, Grandma?"

This time her kiss goes directly on the end of my nose. "She will break a lot of things, helter-skeltering around, making a crazy mess and getting lost. We need to make *both* kinds of choices, my darling, to love our lives and grow wise. A step toward what makes you safe, and then a leap into what can grow you in a new direction."

I think about this for a long time. Well, for me it's a long time. Then I ask, "I get that you have to choose to walk back and forth on each foot, risk and safe, risk and safe, but how do you find the place where the Promise is hidden, and what does it have to do with the Wisdom Trail?"

She spirals our hands around in the air again and explains, "The Promise isn't a place, my darling. It can be hidden for many years, but each time you go around the Wisdom Trail, you find out more and more about what it is and what it isn't."

Now I'm curious. Maybe there will be forests and monkeys and wicked witches like the ones Dorothy found on the Yellow

Brick Road. "So how does the Wisdom Trail help me when I get lost, Grandma?"

She keeps me waiting for a lot of breaths and places her warm palm in the center of my chest while it rises and falls. Finally, she says, "Find the Island of your Heart, because that's where the One Who Listens lives. You'll discover that there are certain questions that your life keeps asking you over and over. Maybe yours will be something like, 'What will make me feel really alive right now? What will make me love being alive in this moment?' Sometimes they'll lead you to take a risk, sometimes to make yourself safe."

I kind of get it. "So Grandma, if I keep finding the Island, then noticing if I'm choosing something to feel alive or safe, I'll find the Promise and not get lost anymore?"

Instead of answering, she points at the bowl sitting on top of the red oilcloth covered table. The dough has risen to touch the towel that covers it, and I know it's time to knead the challah.

Alternate Lifestyle for a Wounded Housewife

It was a time when even Krazy Glue couldn't hold the pieces of Humpty Dumpty's life together. It was a time when doing everything the Princess was supposed to do just wasn't enough. It was a time when all I knew was that I had to get away, away from the imperfectly perfect Fort Lauderdale castle. It was a time when the Imperfectly Perfect Prince had written "I want to be miserable. Leave me alone!" with red lipstick on each of the castle's mirrors and windows and then roared off with all the money in our savings account in my dark green MG Midget. The Princess screamed "no!" into a world without illusion. The world smiled back. It hadn't heard a thing.

It was a time when I stood between a rock and a hard place with a four-year-old son clinging to my leg, terrified. Humans need each other to feel safe. David needed me, and I needed him.

His kindergarten teacher, Pat Sheyer, came over that afternoon to find out why he hadn't come to school. After walking around for a few minutes, she opened her purse, took out her wallet, and then, without saying a word, she hugged each of us, fluttered two hundred single dollar bills over the kitchen floor, and left. I stuffed them into my purse, grabbed my son, and drove our wood-sided Jeep into town. Without having planned what I would do ahead of time, I found myself walking into the office of a magazine that had just started publication. I told Meggie Farley, the managing editor, that I was going to drive around the world with my son for an indeterminate amount of time. "I…um…want to write a column for you about our adventures entitled, 'Alternate Lifestyle for a

Frustrated Housewife.' " I was as surprised as she was when those
words fell out of my mouth.

A month later, a woman dressed in a blue uniform at the airline
ticket counter was asking me where I wanted to go. The future was a
language I no longer spoke. All I could say was, "Away from here."
Maybe I figured it was better for us to be two pilgrims with no
specific destination than to cross the wrong threshold as I had been
doing, year after year.

We spent the first two weeks of our travel holed up in a nice safe
London hotel room, eating meals from room service as we gazed
out at the Marble Arch. At night, David read Tintin books and I
read about possibilities in little red Michelin guidebooks. When he
got bored, I told him stories about all the adventures we were going
to have. When he got antsy, we ran through the long hallways, then
up and down in an old-fashioned elevator. It had a brass handle
that you turned to the right to go up and to the left to go down
and folding metal gates that slid closed and open. If David hadn't
scampered out of those gates at the lobby after a week and then run
out the revolving glass door of the hotel, we might be there still. I, of
course, ran after him in a frenzy, but, when I caught up, he grabbed
my knees and, looking up at me with shining dark eyes, insisted that
we could go any place we wanted if we gave the driver of one of the
big black cars something called shillings. "Do you have shillings,
Mommy? Let's go…someplace else!"

I asked the driver of one of those big black cars to take us to a very
fancy restaurant. We sat up on a white leather banquette with long
mirrors behind us and ate rijsttafel, an Indo Dutch banquet that
didn't have one thing either of us had ever tasted before. David
stuck to the rice and complained that it wasn't as good as Uncle
Ben's. Just as we were finishing, a lean woman in a deep red slinky

velvet dress approached our table. She looked down at me, placed a perfectly manicured ivory hand on my shoulder, and said, "My name is Dora. I just want you to know that if you travel on the Wisdom Trail, you're both going to be just fine." Then she turned on her high-heeled shoes and was gone. David asked me what a "wisdom trail" was, but I was too stunned to answer him. As we prepared to leave, the waiter brought a glass of ginger ale for David and a flute of champagne for me. He told us our dinner bill had been paid.

The next morning, I wrote my first column for the magazine on a brand-new Smith Corona portable typewriter that Pat Sheyer had given to me. Then we were off on the Wisdom Trail, hopping from one Someplace Else to another, from the Marble Arch to the Eiffel Tower, from a pension near the house in central Amsterdam where Anne Frank hid from the Nazis to the sparkling clean tiled Mercedes Benz factory in Stuttgart. I used the last of the money I had from the sale of our Fort Lauderdale house to pay for a shiny white diesel sedan stocked with every spare part that was available, including studded snow tires and Italian air horns that played "La Cucaracha" when a hidden switch under the dashboard was pressed. David decided to name the car "Mutter." I later found out that meant "mother" in German. It seemed appropriate.

He counted twenty-four stitched strips on the right side of Mutter's front leather seat and declared they would be his room. The remaining twenty-four were mine. The entire back seat was his Lego playroom and Tintin comic book library. The enormous trunk was for my precious typewriter, a big red nylon backpack stuffed with two sets of clothes, two novels, an electric converter, a Michelin travel guide, an Army green camera bag stuffed with as much of a pharmacy as I could carry, and a metal foam padded suitcase that held a Nikon camera and assorted lenses. Also snuggled in there was

David's small green backpack, into which a blue tattered sixteen-inch square of Plinkely—his baby blanket—and two pairs of jeans, T-shirts, underpants, and socks had been carefully folded.

Mutter carried us for two years and 50,000 miles across the European continent, the Mideast, Turkey, and down the east coast of Africa, Singapore, China, and throughout Japan. We went from one open moment to another, changing locations at the end of each month in search of moments we loved. Before we left each place, I typed out a column about our adventures and mailed it from the local American Express office, where I also picked up a check from the magazine for the last article as well as a stack of thin blue aerogram letters from my family. Then we bought more Legos, Tintin comic books, and the next red Michelin guide.

We drove through risky, life-threatening intersections, such as through a smallpox epidemic in what was formerly Yugoslavia, where bodies were being burned on the side of the road and the last open border was a twelve-hour drive away. We drove through a small-scale war in Uganda at a time when Idi Amin's crop duster "air force" dropped bombs over the countryside and we cowered in Mutter's back seat.

We drove through Tanzania, where all four tires blew, one after the other, on a hot tarmac road because I had forgotten that the metal studs in the Italian snow tires would expand and then burst. I had to put on the spares surrounded by local people who emerged from the bush murmuring unintelligible words that were neither Swahili nor Masai. When they wouldn't let me back in the car, I shouted to David to grab the Beretta pistol out of the glove compartment and turn on the air horns. "La Cucaracha" blasted out and everyone scattered. I grabbed the gun out of my five-year-old son's hands and locked it securely away again. Every fiber in me was shaking.

David jumped up and down, thrilled at the adventure. After a three hundred-mile drive to the next rest lodge in Mpika on that last spare tire, we collapsed on a small bed. We were both so exhausted that I even ignored the huge black tarantula spider crawling up the tent of mosquito netting we slept under. I was too tired to be scared.

There were exquisite moments of celestial harmony when allies appeared to help us. We traveled from Cape Town to Singapore, Mutter and all, on a tramp steamer. While I vomited in our tiny cabin belowdecks during what seemed like one ongoing storm, the Taiwanese crew tied a rope around David's waist so he wouldn't slide overboard and then taught him how to play Mahjong and Fan-Tan in their kitchen. He began to speak enough basic Cantonese to be understood. I secured another passport so we could follow Nixon into mainland China. Crowds of people gathered around David, stunned at the sight of a white child speaking Cantonese to the pigeons in the local park.

As soon as we had mastered the food, language, and road signs of one country, it was time for another border crossing, another risk in the unknown of a new culture. In northern Japan, I found a lovely small inn, a ryokan. I chose it because Kay-san, the woman in charge, spoke English, rare in this remote village. More importantly, David adored her, probably because she made him things that he liked to eat. We had run out of Captain Crunch in Kyoto, and after weeks of preferring near starvation to fish eyes, searing wasabi, and slimy ginger, the fried chicken and rice she made for him tasted better than the Colonel's. One of the first things he showed her was Plinkely, his tattered piece of baby blanket, which had shrunken until it was no more than a tiny rag. She encouraged him to put it in the sunshine on a window ledge where small brown birds pulled threads from it to make their nests under the roof eaves. One evening, David turned to me and said he was ready to have *his* own nest, a real normal home outside of Mutter. I was struck with terror. How would I ever find a way to stand on my other foot and create stability for us?

Kay-san provided me with a precious respite from the endless questions of his six-year-old mind. I hiked through winter woods where the only sound I had to listen to was snowflakes falling from ancient cedar trees. On one such morning, I followed a line of black-robed monks walking in a single file silently through the trees. They carried a wicker cage between them with a single white dove inside. I followed them up a winding mountain path lined with ancient pine trees. When they reached the top, they gathered in a circle, chanted words I could not understand, opened the cage's small door, and released the bird. It circled above our upturned faces and disappeared. I clicked one shot after another with my wide-angle lens. They folded their hands in their robes and turned to walk back down the path, many with tears glistening on their cheeks. One monk stayed behind and approached me. After bowing, he asked me about the Nikon camera with the big lens that was hanging around my neck. English! I learned from him that these monks were living in a nearby Buddhist monastery and that one of them had just died. Releasing the bird meant that his spirit would fly free on the wings of the dove. He told me they were going to have a special silent *mono no aware* meditation and invited me to join. I had no idea what mono no aware was (or Zen or meditation either). He did his best to explain that it is the awareness that everything in existence is temporary. The monks' tears were not those of grief, but rather a reminder of the preciousness of each moment and the uniqueness of each beautiful life. My grandmother whispered in my mind, "Just so. They too know about the Island of the Heart."

The monk invited me to sit with them in a circle for a few hours. After 50,000 miles with my tempestuous, chattering, wiggling son, three hours of peace, quiet, and stillness seemed like heaven on earth. As we entered the large empty hall, the senior monk, who was called Roshi, knelt by the door and bowed to each of us as we entered the big empty room. One by one, each monk knelt and bowed to him. The Roshi leaned over, reached his thumb into a black lacquered box, and then pressed it to the monk's forehead for just a moment. I was the last in line and kneeled, then bowed as the others had done. He pressed his thumb into the box and then on my forehead. I did my best to quietly walk over to the circle of little wooden stools in the middle of the room. I tucked my stiff dungareed legs under the stool as the Roshi rang a large metal bell shaped like a bowl.

After what seemed like forever noticing a breath then excruciating knee pain, a breath then agonizing shoulder pain, a breath then burning spinal pain, I distracted myself by sneaking a look at the meditating monks around me while pretending not to. I noticed that each of them had a different colored dot pressed into his forehead. I forced my eyes back to the place on the tatami mat in front of me. My mind was racing. What did those dots mean? Did I have one? I must have one. But why? And, most importantly, what color was mine? A long time later, my knees and spine had gone completely numb. I realized that I knew the color of the dot of every monk in the room and they knew mine, but I didn't know my own color. The others couldn't have known their own color either. They must be as curious as I was about the color of their dot. There were, of course, no mirrors. I wrestled with what felt like hot red fire ants crawling in my bone marrow. We were supposed to sit absolutely still. Even twitching and scratching were not allowed. There was nothing left for my mind to do but wander and then wonder. Each time I did, another story emerged about who each monk was, what tragedy had caused him to enter a monastery, and finally what his Promise could possibly be and how he could be realizing it by sitting silently on the floor in the middle of the winter woods of northern Japan. I schemed how to sneeze or cough in such a way that I could surreptitiously scratch my forehead, getting just a bit of color on my nail. Then my thoughts shifted, and I remembered Plinkely and David's request to make a home outside of Mutter. Then I breathed. Then I remembered the Wisdom Trail, and then I found the One who is always there on the Island of my Heart listening. The edges of everything melted.

The gong sounded three times. We all bowed to the center of the room, and then rose to leave, walking very slowly toward the door: one breath, one step. The Roshi was waiting at the entrance. As each monk bowed, he smiled ever so slightly, reached up, and, with a damp handkerchief, wiped off the dot he had placed there three hours before. We bowed again and left, never to discover what every person in that room could see as plainly as the forehead on the front of our face—the color of our dot. I immediately went to the impeccably clean white tiled bathroom and looked closely in the mirror. Not a pore held a hint of any color. I'm not sure what meaning I would have made of a smidgen of blue or a shadow of red anyway.

I began to laugh joyously for the first time in two years and 50,000 miles. I realized I was no longer running away. I realized I was no longer who I'd thought I would grow up to be. I understood that the Promise is like those colored dots and that we need one another to truly discover and enact it. It is more like a constellation than a destination.

So much for the column. In San Diego harbor, I sold my camera, the telephoto lens that had fallen off of the tripod onto a leopard's head one moonlit night in Kenya, the wide-angle lens that had captured the floating life aboard sampans in Singapore. And I sold

Mutter, which paid off the last tramp steamer ticket and enabled me to buy a shiny yellow Volkswagen Beetle. We set off across the country following a spiral trail. It was time for David and me to move toward creating a life we could love, a life where I served others, which was the only way I could really serve myself.

Footsteps to Follow

I thought I was done with kids. For seven decades, my life had been full of them, especially the "odd ones" who no one else wanted to mentor. Now I was an oldster learning to be an elder. I decided to be silent three days a week so I could write this book. I promised myself I wasn't going to mentor anyone anymore, except the Goldendoodle who lives with us.

On one of my few social days, I went out to lunch with two dear friends. Each of us had mothered sons who are or were at some point odd ones. Simona's story bypassed my brain and went directly to my heart. Recently divorced from an abusive man, she was working full time in addition to raising two teenaged sons and a daughter and caring for an aging mother who had metastatic melanoma. They lived in an old house that was literally crumbling at its foundations. The middle boy had been diagnosed with Tourette's syndrome, and the oldest one was just plain lost and barely getting by. "He's such a good kid, but I don't know how to help him find some direction. I'm worried he'll turn out to be a useless alcoholic like his father," she said, tears dripping from the corners of her shockingly blue eyes.

When I finally met Kelly two weeks later, I didn't expect to have to look up so far. He was at least six foot five inches tall, with a chest caved in from stooping over and flashing eyes that made his mother's seem dull in comparison. I had no idea what I could say or do that would be helpful to this seventeen-year-old beanstalk. We had nothing in common. Without the role of teacher or therapist or even mom, I had no preassigned things I was supposed to tell him or do with him. So I decided just to like him. That would have to be enough. I promised myself I'd just spend one little hour listening. I explained all of that to him. Kelly sat down next to me, twined his ridiculously long legs around each other, looked out at the horizon, and replied, "I came over because I don't have anything to lose. But I don't have any money to pay you."

"What can you offer in exchange for my time? You've got a lot of that in front of you. I don't."

His face broke into a smile. "Well, I'm strong and I'm good with plants and stuff like that." His grin lit up the sky. My liking of him grew instantly. We both looked out at my long-neglected backyard.

"OK," I said. "Help me build a garden, and I'll tell you a medicine story you'll never forget. How's that for a deal?"

Kelly leaned forward and asked me what a medicine story was. "Well, you tell me a question that's really hurting you or driving you crazy. Then, I tell you a story that was passed on to me by someone very wise. Then the story works slowly, like medicine in your heart, and helps you live through that question until it doesn't hurt anymore."

He rubbed his stubbled chin. "What if I don't know the right question to ask, or what if I have lots of questions that hurt me?"

"I don't know. You can ask them all, and we'll just see what happens."

Kelly paced around in front of me. "Here goes then. I feel dead inside. I don't ever want to be like my father, or my stepdad for that matter, either. I'm afraid I'll grow up to be an alcoholic. That's in my blood! And I don't want to be a man like my stepfather, who constantly criticizes everyone and tells people what's wrong with them all the time and only thinks about what he can get them to do for him. I don't want to be like my mom either, who's exhausted because she's always thinking about what other people need and never about herself. Besides, she's a woman. So whose footsteps do I follow?"

I just listened, waited, breathed. No story rose over the horizon of my mind. I had noticed that when Kelly was speaking, he habitually seemed to turn his head slightly to the left, as if he was looking backward over that shoulder. I asked, "Given all of that, what's your hurting question?"

He scratched the back of his long neck and shrugged. I waited. Nothing. I waited some more. Finally, he blurted out, "This world is really fucked up, but what can I do about it? What kind of a future will I have if I don't even know how I can make a difference in it?"

I don't know if giraffes can cry, but this long-limbed young man sat down on the ground, folded his legs, and sobbed into his own two hands. I held his question in the stunned silence of my heart and rocked with it. Finally, a story rose from the emptiness. *Once upon a time, in a place not so far from here, in a time not so long ago, psychiatrist Dr. Rachel Naomi Remen, was speaking to a young man who was just about your age, Kelly. He had been diagnosed with juvenile diabetes and had become very self-destructive and full of rage. After six months in therapy with her, he had a most amazing dream: He was sitting facing a small stone statue of the Buddha, young, serene, peaceful. Mind you, he knew nothing about Buddha. Without warning, a dagger was thrown from behind over this young man's left shoulder, lodging itself deep in the Buddha's heart. He felt betrayed, outraged, and in despair, but, as he sat there crying, the statue, ever so slowly, began to grow. It was just as peaceful as before, but it grew and grew until it was enormous, filling the room. The knife remained, but it now was just proportionately the size of a tiny toothpick in the chest of the huge, smiling Buddha. Rachel ends the story by saying that the life force inside each of us can grow stronger than anything that challenges us. It can even free us from what we have to endure. Then she told the young man "Sometimes, someone dreams a dream for us all."*

Kelly leaned back against the chair and looked up at me. "That's a cool story, but I don't get it. What's the medicine for me?"

I waited long enough for his question to float as if it were a balloon. "Every good question deserves another, Kelly. Did you notice the knife came from over his left shoulder? You often look back over *your* left shoulder when you talk about your past. I know you want to be able to think about your future, but it seems to me that what you're most aware of is what's been left out in your past: a father you can respect, guidance from a man who appreciates all you can bring, learning how to set boundaries and reject abuse, and a vision of a future life that you can love."

Kelly stretched out those long legs and inadvertently glanced back over his left shoulder again. A smile crossed his face as he said, "Yup. You're right. That's exactly what I do. Never noticed that before. Doing it makes me wonder whether the future will be just like the past. Since all that was back there was shitty, maybe all that's coming will be shitty too."

Since he was lying stretched out on the floor flat on his back, I could lean over and look down at him. "Try something for me, Kelly. Sit up and look back over your other shoulder. Then tell me everything that was *right* about your history. Tell me what you loved and what you've learned to be good at doing. Tell me how you composted all that shit and what you grew in it. Tell me about what you've learned to care about."

And he did just that. Haltingly at first, but then words poured out about how he had developed a tender heart and how much he loved the earth and wanted to grow things in it, and how he had a pretty good sense of humor and could even make his mother laugh when she was really down. He spilled out his delight in helping other people, even his "gnarly" brother. He lit up talking about surfing and skiing and being in nature, and how someday he wanted to build a house with his own hands on land he owned by the ocean. By the time he had finished, his spine was straight and he was on his feet looking out at the horizon.

"Seems to me that you're growing the Buddha, Kelly. The footsteps you are following are your own." I proceeded to tell him about the trip David and I had taken around the world, making life loving choices. I told him about my grandmother's lesson of finding the one in my mind who is always listening. I leaned over and kissed the top of his head the way my grandmother would have and wished him well as he explored his own Wisdom Trail. Kelly grinned, and the horizon lit up. All in all, it was an hour well spent.

How Do I Risk My Significance?

Tramping up the five floors to Grandma's apartment, all of my thoughts are coated with the smell of yeast and sunlight and flour dust. My short legs can't go as fast as my anticipation, so I mold her face in my mind—the deep caves where her gleaming eyes peer out, the high cheekbones, the webbing of lifelines that make intricate designs in her skin. As I get closer and closer, I can feel her reaching out to me. Even though she's a tiny woman, her hands are large and timeless, with veins that have risen to the surface the way they do on maple leaves.

The climb seems even longer and harder today because my heart is as heavy as a big flat stone. Grandma wears a black dress with a white lace crocheted collar, and, as she opens the door, she sweeps me into her arms. She's like a female spider with a pouch in its belly, from which unravels an endless thread of light and warmth to wrap around me. I can bring her the worst junk in the world, and what she'll do is tie it all up in a neat package and float it in front of us. Then when we take it out on the orange fire escape and snuggle together, she'll help me digest it until I figure out what it needs.

On the street below us, a shiny black car pulls over to the curb and a man steps out dressed in a fancy coat with a raccoon collar and a diamond ring on his pinky finger. I forget completely about the heavy stone. "Look Grandma, look at that rich man. What is he doing in this neighborhood?"

Her lips press together tightly. "I don't think he's really rich, Ketzaleh. If you want to see rich, look down the street at Pauly over there." Pauly is a boy born with no legs who scoots up and down the block on a piece of wood that has roller wheels attached under it. As

the man in the coat turns around, he throws a penny just beyond
Pauly to where he can't reach it, snorts a laugh, and then snarls for
him to get out of his way. "Look deeper at that man, Ketzaleh, look
all the way down to his heart. Are you still sure he's rich?"

I do as she tells me. All I can see is shadow. Before I can say
anything, she tells me to look at Pauly's heart. I see him wheel over
to the penny, stretch over, and then put it in his pocket. He beams at
the man in the coat and says, "I really want you to have a good day,
mister." Pauly's like that. He blesses everybody and everything that
crosses his path. In fact, I call him "The Blessing Boy."

"Pauly's heart is gold," said Grandma. "That's why he shines so.
He's the one who's truly rich. Now tell me, Ketzaleh, what is this
heaviness you brought to me today?" She points in front of us
instead of in my chest to remind me we can study it if it's out there
instead of inside my body.

I put the warm palm of her hand over my face so I can smell the
yeast for comfort. "Mommy says I'm a liar and I should be ashamed
of myself. She told me that Daddy's gonna spank me for my own
good when we get home tonight. She said the Girl Scout leader
called her and said I was kicked out of the troop because I kept
telling all the other girls stories about lights I saw around them.
Mommy says I have to stop exaggerating and telling stories because
what would people think if they knew I was a little liar. That makes
my heart hurt, and that's really what Mommy said. I'm not making
that up, Grandma."

By this time, her arms are wrapped around me, and I sob into her
black dress while she rocks back and forth. I blow my nose in her
white handkerchief embroidered with little pink flowers in the
corner and listen to her whispery words. "Ketzaleh, you need to

know that your mother just doesn't understand about your Promise. She would think that the man in the fur coat is rich and that Pauly was wrong to be in his way. She worries all the time about what other people think, including people like your Girl Scout leader."

"So Grandma, are you saying that telling stories is really part of my Promise, and that Mommy doesn't know what it is and the Girl Scout leader doesn't either? Is that what you are telling me?"

She straightens my red braids and touches the center of my chest. "We're always challenged about our Promise. That's meant to help us make it strong and learn to use it well."

"So when I tell stories and do what Mommy calls 'exaggerating,' I'm really being challenged where the Promise lives in my heart—like how Pauly was challenged by being yelled at by the man in the coat. Is that right?"

"Just so, Ketzaleh. You don't need to hide the stories that bubble in your heart. You just need to know that your mother doesn't understand this. Her Promise is about taking care of other people."

I nod, thinking of how my mother insists that everything must be neat and exactly right like a photograph.

"So she doesn't understand that I think by asking questions and telling stories and that's a good thing? No one else does either, not my Daddy or my sister, and certainly not the Girl Scout leader. Ever. But you do, Grandma. Right?"

She places a sweet soft kiss on the center of my forehead and releases a long slow sigh. "Perhaps keeping you safe is part of your mother's Promise. Maybe she and your father and sister and even the Girl Scout leader care too much about what other people think, or care in the wrong way."

"How can you care in the wrong way, Grandma?"

"If you care in a way that makes you forget about being true to your heart, that's the real lie. That makes a person feel dark and heavy inside." She reaches over and puts my palm on the center of my chest and continues, "That's a lot to think about, Ketzaleh, and a lot to understand, I know, but just remember to put your hand on your heart like this whenever the Promise feels heavy and tell it you'll find a way to let it grow. Someday it will fly free like the pigeons. Thank it and bless it like Pauly does. Now, shall we go and make some bread?"

"OK, Grandma, but one last question. Is the Promise a bird? Can it fly above all the poop and bad stuff?"

Grandma points one finger at a pigeon on the fire escape. "Do you see how it has two wings? One wing helps you see what really is true and that gives you wisdom. The other helps you imagine what could be and that gives you inspiration."

"Like us, right? You're wise, and I imagine things. Together we make a pigeon!"

"Maybe. And maybe the Promise is a bird with one wing that can make up stories and the other that can help you fly above the poop and see when and where the best time and place is to tell your stories! Now, let's get ready for the Sabbath."

Let Wounds Be My Teachers

I was born shortly after Pearl Harbor was attacked and grew up between the stunning parentheses of two predominant images: the mushroom-shaped cloud over Hiroshima and the first view of the glowing green earth as a whole, photographed from space by an astronaut. Until I was in my late twenties, I did what I was taught to do: master questions by pursuing the right answers. This allowed me to believe that I knew more than most people. It gave me diplomas to hang on the wall, degrees printed in a fancy font that proved I knew something important and that I was entitled to make a living by giving answers to others. This also gave me the illusion of mastery, security, identity, and control. One ordinary June day, I found myself stranded on the edge of an eroding cliff, with all those answers shredded and useless in a wind I could no longer control.

All the people on my mother's side of our family grew lumps somewhere in their bodies. My Aunt Chuch had one in her spine that grew until it eventually killed her. My sister had one on her nose that was benign, and another in her brain that wasn't. It, too, grew until it eventually killed her. When I was thirty, a malignant lump grew on my spleen and metastasized. I had just returned from driving around the world for two years with David. We moved into a tiny apartment on Poverty Lane in West Lebanon, New Hampshire, where I tried to make plans for David's future and my own demise.

Cancer brought me to my knees. I could neither ignore it nor run from it. The people around me kept encouraging me to fight. But I'd never even won a fight with a mosquito. I knew flight. I knew how to freeze. But fighting, even with something that was trying to take my life, was completely foreign to me. Cancer galloped faster than I could think. I found myself at the very edge of what it means to be a human being: vulnerable, fragile, and impermanent. It dug away at everything that was supposed to be solid. At night, after putting my six-year-old to sleep, I snuck outside and threw my arms around a big maple tree. It absorbed my tears, screams, fear, and hopelessness. I can still feel the bark of that old tree on my cheek.

The "expertocracy" at Dartmouth Medical School inundated my mind with diagnoses that explained how the cells growing so creatively throughout my system would soon take over and kill me. I thought this meant I had failed. Friends suggested that I should try chemicals that would poison me at a cellular level; long-distance healers mumbled incantations to cleanse me of the effects of many missteps I had taken that had caused the cancer to grow in the first place. Other practitioners suggested I visualize, meditate, carry crystals that would change my vibrational level, and allow various entities to help me move beyond fear to a kind of bravery I couldn't even imagine. Under all of these suggestions was the implication that I had somehow brought cancer upon myself. My reaction was an impotent rage. I wanted nothing more than to place my fingers around their well-meaning throats and squeeze tight. Luckily, there were so many tubes running fluids into my arms that I couldn't even fight the advice that was, after all, for my own good.

I flew to a specialist whose office was on Park Avenue in New York City. My mother had taught me that when you're sick, you deserve the best. Therefore, any doctor on Park Avenue had to be the best. His office furniture was dark brown leather. He puffed on a carved meerschaum pipe while explaining that no one had ever recovered from the kind of cancer I "had." Then he told me my life expectancy was three months, more or less, so I'd better make arrangements for my son.

His partner, a surgeon at Columbia Presbyterian Hospital,
suggested that he could relieve some of the pain I was experiencing
by removing one of the "lumps," but not to get my hopes up because
it wasn't going to change the "terminal" outcome.

The first night after surgery, a Jamaican angel disguised as a
nurse's aide in a green uniform put her broom against the wall
and sat her heavy body down in the turquoise plastic chair next
to my bed. She brought no treatments, no fixes. She didn't put
anything into my body or take anything from it, even when I was
moaning from excruciating pain and frozen in fear. She just sat
and attended me, her warm hand on my foot, her breath like the
tides of the Caribbean. She left two words on the shore of my mind:
"As is, darling. As is." I had no idea what these words meant, but
the sound of her breath became a gentle tide, carrying me like a
luminescent jellyfish.

My angel returned each night, repeating the same ritual. I listened
for the sound of her broom sweeping the halls, waited for the
comfort only she could bring. One evening she added a question to
those three words. "What if you are more than that pain, more than
that fear, darlin'?"

My breath slowed to match hers. I couldn't answer that question,
I could only float on it like that jellyfish. Even though it has no
muscles, it isn't afraid. Weak as it is, the jellyfish can be carried by
the might of the entire ocean flowing through it. My Jamaican angel
had given me much more than two words and a healing question.
I began to search for other questions that opened my attention
so I could float around with them on the bottom of the sea: What
if the healing of my heart is as important as the healing of my
body? How can I learn to relate to the things I can't control? How

can I influence cancer and fear even though I may not be able to control them?

I read everything I could find. One blessed afternoon in the Dartmouth College library, I literally stumbled over an old copy of *Man's Search for Meaning* by a psychologist named Victor Frankl. I decided to take it home even though I wasn't a man and I wasn't searching for meaning, just a way to live. But the first few pages revealed that he had survived life in a concentration camp. None of my relatives had ever done that, and the cancer diagnosis certainly felt like Auschwitz, so I dug in, searching for inspiration. I read how he had learned to open his heart in hell by discovering "personal freedom." I learned that no one else could take away my right to choose the meaning I ascribed to any event that happened to me. The gates of my mind blew wide open with a clean and clearing wind. If I could learn to become comfortable in the unknown, I could choose which stories I told myself about what was going on in my body and what I was and was not capable of and responsible for.

A friend told me about a Russian Israeli physicist named Moshe Feldenkrais who'd founded a system of psychophysical reeducation. I had no idea what that meant. I've always been a learning junkie, but I was hooked on the "psycho" rather than the "physical." Since that was what was now growing uncontrollably, what did I have to lose? I flew to San Francisco for a weekend workshop. There were about eighty people in the room, most of them therapists and body workers from Esalen. Moshe was bald, built like a mountain, and spoke with a thick accent. He told us to fold our hands habitually, as we had done all of our lives while trying to behave. Then he asked us to notice how we had done that. Were the right fingers in front of the left or the left in front of the right? Next, he asked us to unfold them, keeping them open in wonder for a minute or two and then reweaving them in the opposite, non-habitual way. We folded, held open, wondered and refolded for several minutes, habitual to wonder to non-habitual to wonder to habitual, while he asked us questions. "Which way feels more comfortable, easier?"

My hands gave me the answer immediately. "Habitually."

"Which way feels safer?"

Again, the answer was obvious. "Habitually."

"Which way are you more aware of the spaces between your fingers, of your bones and the feel of your skin?"

This was getting interesting. "Non-habitually."

"And which way are your hands more alive to you?"

I was stunned. "Non-habitually."

Moshe took us one more step. "Now reconsider which way your hands are safer. Which way could you move more quickly to get them out of the way if they were in danger?"

I kept folding and refolding in wonder. I couldn't believe it. Obviously, my hands were safer if I was more aware of them, and obviously, I was more aware of them if I folded them non-habitually! But I had spent most of my life finding the easy, comfortable, habitual way, avoiding what was awkward at any cost, believing somehow that this was making me safe. Instead, it was making me dead.

Two years later, I was still alive. I rolled around on the floor each morning, exploring the sensations in my body, then danced them, drew them in a large black journal, and made up a story about the drawing. I went back to visit the doctor on Park Avenue. He told me I must have gone into a remission of some kind because no one ever survived the form of cancer I had been diagnosed with. I asked if he was interested in what I had done. He shook his head no, lit his meerschaum pipe and explained that he was an old man and would be retiring soon. All of his patients had died. If there was something that *could* have helped them, he'd never be able to forgive himself, so it was best I not tell him. I left his fancy office stunned into silence, shaking my head.

Cancer has returned as a teacher six times since that first visitation As I write these words four and a half decades later, I pause to fold and refold my hands. I've become an expert in living through that awkward space between the comfortable familiarity of the known and all of the alive possibility that waits, ungainly and unknown, on the other side. In between the two, I hang open, wondering, floating in an ocean of wisdom, remembering that the Promise deep within me has all the buoyancy I need. The muscles in my body with its "unhealed disease" unclench, remembering the many things my body has done right: grown and given birth to a child, driven around the world for two years when he was four, written various books, including this one, and told more stories than even my overactive imagination can hold onto.

That Which Is Unfinished for Me to Give

I didn't plan to do a session with him. All of my professional energy
was absorbed by writing. But Sal was a dear friend, and I was very
concerned about how his treatment was affecting the end of his life.
He was a brilliant engineer who had been struggling with pancreatic
cancer. For two years, he had flown to several different healing
centers and had gone through endless rounds of chemotherapy,
radiation, hyperbaric chambers, homeopathy, hydration, and
naturopathy. He swallowed handfuls of pills daily, including
steroids, and was experiencing emotional swings of uncharacteristic
gloom or angry explosions directed at his wife Beth.

I mumbled to myself that no one wants to spend the last months of
a life like this. The self in my head mumbled back that his treatment
was "none of my business." But the self in my guts disagreed
vehemently. I'd lived an unhealed life long enough to know that
such suffering can be a call for the companionship of simple
wisdom. My gut intuition won the argument, and I sent him a brief
email inviting him over for a cup of tea and an afternoon of what
the Hawaiians call "talk story."

"Chicken poop" seemed out of place; the moment called for
elephant poop or maybe even dragon poop. I asked Sal if he had
spoken to any other people who had lived with cancer for a long
time. He told me he hadn't and was grateful for the invitation. He
wanted to know what I had done to beat it. Before I could respond,
he told me he didn't intend to stop fighting because he had several
projects at work that only he could complete. I explained that I
hadn't beaten anything but that I'd be very willing to tell him about
my own experience. He nodded and leaned forward.

I whispered, "As is" to myself, and then I allowed stories to unfurl as they came. "Until cancer came into my life, I made my living by being rationally intelligent. I expected every problem to have a solution and every question to have an answer. But cancer was a teacher not at all impressed with that kind of intelligence."

Sal leaned in a few inches closer, so I continued, "Before I got sick, I was so busy trying to finish my never-ending list of things to do that I forgot to notice the moments I was living—the feeling of the wind against my cheek or the sunlight gleaming on my son's hair. But when I was labeled terminally ill and began this journey I call 'cancering,' a profound shift happened in my mind. Things that minutes before had seemed urgent lost their meaning completely, while people or issues I had pushed to the bottom of the list became supremely important."

I looked up and Sal was nodding, so I continued. "Faced with the razor's edge of impending death, all of my assumptions were shredded. My center of balance shifted. My mind wanted things to stay just as they had always been. My spirit knew I was going to lose everything anyway, so I decided to enjoy each second that was available, no matter what. I could feel a life force at the very center of my being, a longing, a truth that wanted to be expressed somehow. Living what I call the unlived life became more important than anything else."

Sal sipped his tea and encouraged me to go on. "In the beginning, I ran from one cure to another, chased by the belief that I had somehow created the cancer. Ultimately, that led me to complete despair. The drugs I was taking turned my words into knives. Anger seemed to be my only option. Fight the cancer. Fight anything and anyone that got in the way of my cure. But since I couldn't

'think' my way through this battle, I felt helpless and impotent like
never before."

I paused, and Sal told me how he felt caught in the middle of
a seesaw, with anger forcing him to shout at his wife and fear
compelling him to withdraw into a place in his mind that was like
a prison cell. "All I seem to be able to do is to turn against or turn
away from everything. So I turn toward my list and try to get all of
my work finished."

I breathed slowly. "A story just floated into my mind, Sal, that I'd
like to share with you. Is that OK?" After he nodded, I said: *There
was a group of concentration camp inmates at Buchenwald who were
clinging to the dark corners of a concrete block room waiting to be
taken into the gas chamber. They had been stripped of their ragged
black and white striped uniforms and huddled close to one another.
One man had saved a single sheet of tattered paper that he then
shredded into enough thin strips so that each person could have one.
Someone else had sneaked in a stump of a pencil. Passing it around,
each inmate wrote a one-line message on the strip, curled it tightly,
and tucked it into a crack between the blocks in the wall. When the
camp was liberated months later, the messages were found.*

"Ever since I heard this story, Sal, I've wondered what I would have
written on my scrap."

Sal sat back in the chair, eyes glazed over as if he were looking
through me. Then he shook his head. "I'm pretty smart, but I don't
even know how to begin thinking about that."

"When you and I were young kids, Sal, we were spontaneous and
free in our minds. Cancering made me wonder how I had become
so stiff and encrusted. How did I cut myself off from all of the wild

beauty that's in the world? Am I a prisoner like those inmates, or
is freedom something else altogether? Is it a way of thinking? Is
it a verb, rather than something I have or don't have, or a thing I
can earn? What if I just floated in the questions I can't answer and
wondered instead? What if I am really more than my fear? What
would I write on that tiny scrap of paper?"

Sal slumped into the back of the wicker rocking chair. Shaking his
head slowly, he closed his eyes. I decided to continue.

"A very wise man named Thomas Carlyle said that the tragedy of
life isn't so much what humans suffer as it is what they miss. I no
longer think of cancer as an enemy I have to battle. In my mind
now, it's a teacher who comes to bring me questions that can't be
answered directly but can open my mind and heart. It insists I don't
miss out on loving what's really essential to me. All I can do is hold
the questions lightly, open my attention the way I did as a child,
and float with them as if they were kites. What I've learned to do is
notice what's around me in the moment to love, open my mind, and
pray that I'll grow forward."

Sal rocked back and forth in the chair. Without opening his
eyes, he asked in a soft voice, "So what are the questions that are
carrying you now?"

I waited before responding, the way my grandmother and the
Jamaican angel had waited. Then I leaned toward him and
shared my questions one by one as if they were fireflies on a dark
summer night: "What would I write on that scrap of paper? What's
unfinished for me to give? What's unfinished for me to experience?
What's unfinished for me to learn? What else do I need to do to
realize the Promise life made to the world the moment I was born?
How can I love the life I am living?"

His breath dropped into his belly. I reached over and placed my open palm on the center of his chest and whispered, "Even here, even now, how can love grow?"

What Is Bigger Than My Fear?

Since there are always so many people in Grandma's cramped
Hell's Kitchen apartment, the only place we can be alone and
uninterrupted together is the fire escape outside the living room
window. What I long for more than anything is "just us" so I can
study the designs time has etched on her cheeks, feel her tender
kisses, and slip inside the bubble of one of her enthralling tales. To
get to that fire escape though, I have to climb over the windowsill,
cling to the brick wall, and try not to look down on the street below
while my feet creep along the ledge.

I really, really want to ask her a question today, but I'm too afraid
to do that clinging and creeping. In spite of being old, she moves
nimbly over the sill in her clunky black shoes with the little pinholes
all over them and turns back toward me. She stretches out her long-
fingered hand and calls out, "Come, Ketzaleh, bring your fear with
you. You both will be fine."

Even though I hear her words and believe every one of them, terror
has me frozen in place. "Grandma, I only have one question. I'll
stay here inside and ask you: How will I recognize the Promise if
it can't talk to me? How will I know it's truly the Promise that's
calling to me?"

She sits down and whispers something. The pigeons are cooing so
loudly I can't hear her words. I want to know what she just said
more than anything, so I lean over the sill, stretch my grubby fingers
out to her gnarly ones, and lift one leg over. Then the other one.
Finally, I can cuddle into her side, tears rolling down my cheeks.

"Ah, good. Warm tears. That means your fear is melting,
drop by drop."

"But Grandma, I didn't hear what you said. How will I recognize the
Promise if it can't speak English?"

She kisses the top of my head. "The Promise doesn't speak in words,
darling. It speaks to you through your body. It's like—how do you
say it in English—it's like a longing."

Longing? I have no idea what that word means.

"A minute ago, your fear was very strong. It made you frozen so
that even when you wanted to come out here to sit with me, you
couldn't move. But you must have felt something in your body that
was stronger than your fear. What was that?"

It takes me a minute to remember. Then I answer, "It was
something in the center of my chest where my heart is—something
like a hot hand reaching out and wanting to be close enough to you
so I could hear what you said."

The corners of her mouth twitch into a smile. "Just so. That's what
longing feels like. Some people call it passion. It's like a fire, for sure.
Most people try to ignore their longing because they're afraid it will
get them in trouble. But the trouble really comes when it shrivels up
or bursts out of control."

"Like if I hadn't come out here or if I'd just jumped over the
windowsill without looking or holding on?"

Another kiss lands, this time in the middle of my forehead. "Just so
again. If you pay attention to the longing and listen to it, its warmth

will grow like bread dough in the bowl. It can help you live your yesses, and, even more importantly, it can help you live your no's so you can protect yourself and what you love."

"So should I knead it like you do to the dough?"

"Oh, my darling, you're so smart. Yes, put the love in your hands and knead it. Ask what it needs so it can rise. Check on it every once in a while. Then braid it into your life the best you can. It'll grow bigger than your fear, just like it did when you climbed over that windowsill. So put love in your hands and make something with the longing. It doesn't matter what—a story, a dress, a loaf of bread."

Another question rises that I can't resist. "Grandma, what if I'm doing that and my mind drifts off and I think about something else, like pigeon poop, and the love sifts out of my hands? What then?"

She lifts both of my palms to her lips. Placing a kiss in the center of each, she explains, "All you need to do is begin to think about someone you love or something you love, and your hands will be full of sweet longing again. That's the secret."

No Matter What

The roar I heard in our driveway was not that of a lion in Kenya, but rather a yellow motorcycle spitting gravel beneath its tires as it raced up our driveway in Norwich. The light wasn't the blazing African sun, but rather blue-white Vermont moonlight. It was four in the morning, and I was standing with my back against the front door and all of David's clothes stuffed into the battered green duffel bag at my feet. He pulled up in front of me and dropped one foot on the ground, revving the engine but not saying a word. He was beyond my reach. The beast inside me rose into my chest and out of my mouth, growling, "Whose motorcycle is that? Do you know what time it is!?" I immediately told myself that was a dumb question parents use when they are about to explode. He'd learned to tell time in London staring at Big Ben out of our hotel window when he was four.

Rather than look at his watch, David rolled his eyes, then spit through his braces onto the gravel between us. He'd taken to clearing his throat and spitting a lot lately. At first, I thought it was a teenage boy thing. Maybe his voice was changing, but as far as I could tell he hadn't shown the slightest indication of puberty except for an unbearable, intolerable, impossible, passive-aggressive nastiness.

"It's Mark Canfield's. He bought it with his inheritance money, and he lent it to me so I could come home. Your eyes are all beady and mean. Why are you so pissed off? Just stop being such a bitch!"

I fell back against the front door. Something solid. Yes. I imagined I was falling into the arms of women—many women. My mother. My Aunt Chuch. My Aunt Ruthie. My grandmother. "No more." Two syllables. I'd been trying to learn to say these two simple words for over a year—or my whole life. No more, Daddy, no more hitting! No more men on the street, no more humiliating me by yelling out things about my body! No more, stranger, no more raping me! No more, Steve, no more sex with my best friend in our bed! Even though I knew it was just my son on the motorcycle, not all those men, I also knew I had to make a boundary that very moment. "This has to stop. It stops here, David. No more."

He revved the Yamaha's engine again and shouted, "What the fuck are you talking about, Mom? So I'm a little late, what's the big deal? Why are you so psycho?"

I could hear echoes of all those women in my blood insisting, "It has to stop here, Dawna. No more. Stop him here. Stop him now."

"What you've been doing is not OK, David. It stops here...with you and me." I was vibrating more than the Yamaha's engine. Tears fell down my cheeks as if they were a hot wet curtain. I bent down and picked up the duffel bag and held it against my chest as I spoke, "It's not just what you do, Dave, it's what you DON'T do—you don't go to classes, you don't go to the job I got you, you don't come home when you say you will, you don't do chores, you don't do homework, you don't clean up after yourself!" I was clutching the duffel bag as if it were a swaddled infant, then I extended it out to him. "If you aren't willing to follow the rules of this house, *my* rules, and treat me with respect, then you're out of here, on your own." I released the bag and it tumbled onto the gravel between us.

"What are you talking about? What do you mean that I'm on my own? You're my mother. You *have* to take care of me. You just prefer that new boyfriend of yours to me, that's all!" He revved the motorcycle so loud that my horse in the pasture began to gallop around, terrified.

I imagined him ten years hence on death row, telling a prison therapist that he had savagely killed thirty-seven women in Boston because his mother wouldn't take care of him. But I couldn't back down again. "If you want to live here, David, you have to follow my rules. If you think you're ready to make your own rules, then here's the two hundred dollars in child support money your father sends me every month, and you're on your own. No more abuse. I've had enough!" My foot, with a mind of its own, kicked the duffel bag toward him. My hands shook, my heart shook. I was sure he'd yield any minute, sure he'd climb off the cycle and throw his arms around me, begging for my forgiveness the way he had done each time I rehearsed this moment in my mind. There was no reason to believe he wouldn't.

David was not at an age of reason. He twisted his hand fiercely on the handlebar, and the cycle spun out and around his outstretched foot. For a moment I thought he was going to run me over, but he slowed just enough to reach down and grab the bag and then the check from my hand. The Triumph accelerated toward the pasture. The bluish moonlight made it all seem surreal, as if in slow motion. He drove the motorcycle right through the electric fence, charging Dusty, who galloped to the far corner of the field. She reared up with her eyes rolled back in her head. Without pausing, the motorcycle veered to the left, careened back through the fence again, and sped past me down the driveway. I could hear the engine shift gears as David roared down Beaver Meadow Road. I stood in the cold darkness and listened to the sound of my son racing out of my life.

My mother and sister had told me that giving birth would be the worst pain I'd ever feel, but not to worry because I'd soon forget it. My grandmother said it would be the hardest work I would ever do. It was, except that afterwards, all I could remember was the joy, the luminous miracle of knowing that what was right about all that hard work was the realization that the universe was a friendly place after all because David had been born into it. This night was like giving birth a second time, except there was only pain, with no miracle afterwards. I sobbed for forty-eight hours, muttering, "What's bigger than this, Grandma?"

This was before anyone talked about "tough love." This was even before Oprah Winfrey or Geraldo. This was when people expected families to have two parents with mothers who picked up their sons each day outside a red brick school building. And this was when a mother who taught at a prestigious New England college and trained psychotherapists was never supposed to kick a son out of the family home. Weeks went by. Everything that had ever been straight bent crooked. Finally, my bloodshot eyes cleared enough to read. I wasn't sure my mind could follow, but I grabbed the first book off my shelf that I could reach and opened it to the following story:

Long ago, but not so very far away, there was a young man named Milarepa. He wanted more than anything to find his purpose, so he left his home and traveled around the world. He had many adventures and met several wise teachers. When his face began to crease with age, he decided it was time to return to his birthplace. As he approached the little hut, the doors and windows flew open and hundreds of noxious, hideous demons streamed out, shrieking. Milarepa turned, about to run, but he stopped, remembering that he was home. There was no place else to go. He breathed deeply and bowed to the demons in respect. In the next moment, half of them disappeared. Those that remained screamed even louder. Without

thinking or knowing why the demons were there, Milarepa opened
his heart and out came a song of welcome. As his music surrounded
them, all the rest of the demons disappeared, except for one. He was
the nastiest and most disgusting looking of them all. His breath stank
of sulphur, his eyes bulged in fury, and his hands clawed the sky. Still,
Milarepa moved toward him without hesitation, arms outstretched.
The demon opened his mouth wide to reveal fangs as sharp as knives.
Milarepa whispered to him, "Please help me. I want to understand
your pain and your longing." And then, in the time it takes a
snowflake to melt, the demon was gone. Milarepa was home at last.

I remembered what Grandma had told me about longing. I put all
the love I felt for Dave into my hands and sat down so I could write
a letter to him: nothing dramatic, mind you, just a sweet memory
of a time when, at five years old, he skied for the first time down a
steep slope in Cortina. I asked him to tell me what it was like to be
him right now and what he was longing for.

Each morning I wrote another letter. I had heard he was living at
one of his friends' house and was paying room and board with the
child support checks. I drove past him every afternoon at Dan and
Whit's, the general store, where he had gotten a job pumping gas.
Each time he saw me, he turned his back. My heart contracted with
another labor pain. Nonetheless, I continued to turn my longing
to ink and wrote another letter each day. I hiked down the long
driveway, past the field through which he had roared away, to the
white mailbox with a little red flag for two weeks. Each day, one of
my letters sat inside returned and unopened. Nonetheless, I made
that daily pilgrimage, following in the wake of my longing. And
then, one day, the mailbox was empty. He stopped returning my
letters. Maybe he was even reading them. I continued for three
months of empty. Finally, on an autumn Saturday, bright as it can
only be in Vermont, I could see the upright red flag from my front

door. I galloped down to it, and a scribbled postcard waited for me, inviting me to have brunch the following day with him.

When he approached me at the red leather booth in Lou's Diner, I had to look up. He was taller than before, probably taller than I would be if I stood up, which I didn't. He greeted me casually, and I could hear that his voice had dropped an octave. He told me he had bought his own car, a twenty-year-old Opel convertible. We negotiated over blueberry waffles. He drank glass after glass of Idlenot milk from a plastic gallon jug he had brought with him. By the time the waitress cleared our plates, we were each and both ready for him to move back into our house until he went to college. This time, he was truly standing on his own two huge feet. And so was I.

Perhaps all of that would have happened if I hadn't kicked him out. Perhaps "trustworthy" would still have been the word everyone who knows him uses to describe David thirty-seven years later. Perhaps we would still have ended up growing as close as a mother and son possibly can be. Perhaps.

The Other Side of Everything

I was sitting in a circle of a hundred women. We'd gathered for a
week of silent meditation and meaningful conversation with author
and philosopher Joanna Macy. I was there to grieve my sister's
recent passing. We were all there to repurpose our lives.

There were designs and patterns carved around Joanna's eyes like
those around my grandmother's. She spoke softly, slowly, distinctly,
her words carrying a kind of dignity that can never be trespassed
upon and a kind of compassion that is wider than any violation. She
asked us to form as a circle into what she called a Truth Mandala.
Walking slowly, as if her bare feet were treading on moss, she
stepped from one quadrant of the room to another, dropping
an object in each, explaining that they represented one of four
emotions: anger, fear, despair, and sorrow. Returning to the center
of the circle, she named it the place of truth.

"Each of these emotions has a hidden partner. The other side of
anger is passion. The other side of fear is courage. The other side
of despair is rebirth, and the other side of sorrow is love." She
paused, as if allowing a moment for her words to sink in, and
then continued, "Each of you who wishes to participate, come one
at a time into the center of the circle. Stand in the quadrant that
represents the emotion you need to talk from. Please speak only
from the truth of your own experience. The rest of you…" she
said, turning slowly, "are here with and for one another. Be a sister,
bearing witness for the woman in the center."

I had no intention of speaking. I'd already been public, working far
too much lately. And being a sister, after my own had just died of
brain tumors and agony, seemed more than I could bear. I was raw,

skinless, broken open. I had come to this retreat to crawl into the
concave surface of my heart so I could curl up and lick my wounds.
I sat listening to the other women for over two hours, doing my
best to absorb the stories and hold each one in the cradle of my
attention. I knew how to do this. I had done this with my own sister
for so many months.

The last woman to speak was dressed in reds and oranges like a
living flame, with skin as dark as burnt wood. I thought to myself,
"Panther!" A fury flared through her as she screamed that none
of us could understand what it felt like to be a black woman in
America. Pointing around the circle, she hissed, "Don't tell me you
are my sister. You are not my sister."

When she sat down on the other side of the circle, a torrent broke
inside my chest as if all the frozen rivers in Vermont had cracked
open at once on a warm afternoon. I was lifted on its current and
transported into the center of the circle. A flood of words rushed
through me, carrying the debris of my fifteen-year-old self. She
had been violated in every opening of her body by a man she didn't
know. I was not speaking words now—they were raging through
me. "Passion is the other side of anger? Courage is the other side
of fear? Rebirth is the other side of despair? Love, the other side of
sorrow?" Each question crashed against the shore of the women
sitting around me. "Well, then, tell me, all of you, tell me, what is
the other side of rape?"

The voice that was birthing itself through my throat was not only
my voice. It flowed from Dachau, and the Sudan, from Bosnia and
Harlem and Baghdad, and Michigan and Los Angeles. It rose and
roared from the hundred and sixty million "untouchables" in India
called the Dalits, "those broken to pieces." The current carried me
across the floor from quadrant to quadrant and then at last to the

center of the circle. I turned to face the dark-skinned woman who had spoken before me. I pointed my index finger directly at her. Words raged through that resonated from every fiber of my body. "And... You... You *are*...my...sister!"

Panther woman's arms opened, and she rushed to embrace me. "What is the price of innocence? How much was our childhood worth?" I sobbed. In the circle of her arms, I realized that I'd exiled my soul from my body on the evening my body was raped. I needed to have some part of me that could not be violated. It had lifted out like the pigeons on Grandma's fire escape. It had hidden outside my body in a wall built by silent shame. I learned that from my mother. I learned it from my sister, who had told me she never felt hurt because she locked all those feelings away in a vault in her brain where they couldn't bother her.

Panther woman sobbed with me, shook with me, because she too was remembering being paralyzed by shame and the fear of humiliation. She had been disconnected from the pulsing cells of her body. Re-membering, our separate hearts, each a refugee, found their twin. We nested in each other's possibilities.

"Why do we do this to one another?" Panther woman whispered.

A voice I hadn't allowed to speak for decades said, "When am *I* the perpetrator? What are the broken pieces in my life that I've made untouchable? What do I hide and degrade? What is the longing, the passion in my own heart that I have silenced?"

The other women of the circle stood behind us, arms and hands creating a refuge, a sanctuary. Joanna joined too, saying, "In sharing our stories, we will make the kind of silence that almost suffocated each and all of us obsolete. We are unlearning to not speak."

Panther Woman said in a reverberating voice, "Ashé! We will
make things change!" I stood next to her in the center of the circle,
entwining the fingers of my left hand in her right and raising them
above our heads as if she were a sister of my heart. I called out,
"May it be so!"

All of the women interlaced fingers and we turned the circle
outward, shouting "Ashé! May it be so!" The words fell into the
center of my chest, where they nested. Panther Woman and I
knew we were now what poet John O'Donohue calls *anam cara,*
friends of each other's souls, bigger than any fear, no matter what,
companions to each other's longing.

Braiding

66

*"Joy is the gift of love. Grief is the price of love.
Anger is the force that protects that which
is loved… To be revolutionary, love must be
poured in three directions: toward others,
toward our opponents, and toward ourselves.
Revolutionary love is the call of our times."*

—**Valerie Kaur**

How Do I Grow My Heart?

It's New Year's. Not the New Year's Eve when you get to drink
champagne, but New Year's for Jews, Rosh Hashanah, when I get
to drink sweet dark purple wine from a special silver cup and make
potato pancakes with Grandma. She's told me this is a time to
forgive one another and ourselves for the ways we have messed up
in the past year. Limping up the stairs to her apartment, I stumble
when I think about forgiving others and rub the bandage on my
left shin. The doctor had to sew a whole bunch of ugly stitches
there because Stupid Stevie Silverman forced me to ride on the
front of his two-wheeled bike. One of the spokes broke, and it kept
cutting into my leg. Blood gushed out all over my fancy white lace
socks. I hate Stevie Silverman because he bosses everybody around,
especially girls, especially me. I'm never going to forgive him, even if
Grandma says I should.

Polishing two silver candlesticks for tonight's special dinner, she
stops long enough to place a kiss on her fingertips and press it
gently onto my bandage.

"The doctor had to use black thread to sew it all up and said I'll have
a scar there for the rest of my life. It's all Stupid Stevie Silverman's
fault!" I pout, trying to make her feel so sorry for me that she'll
forget to ask me to forgive him for Rosh Hashanah.

Grandma looks right into my eyes and says, "Ketzaleh, it's special
that you'll have your very first scar. Did you know scars are made
of the strongest tissue in your body? They prove we can grow from
our wounds."

I shake my head. "It's weird that from such a terrible thing as ripping open a leg, my body can grow the toughest thing, Grandma. I have a different question for you, though. Is Stupid Stevie Silverman's Promise that he will be the boss of me? Why do boys think they can boss girls around?"

Grandma doesn't answer at first. She places her left arm around my waist and walks me over to the big table where we'll have dinner. Grandma lifts one silver eyebrow as she looks at me to make sure I'm giving her my attention. I think maybe she's forgotten about my question, but she gets right to it. "No one's Promise could ever be to boss around another person, my darling. What happens is boys are taught that they have to use just the facts in their heads and the strength in their bodies to be men. They're trained to decide who is right and who is wrong. Girls, on the other hand, are taught to use the flexibility in their heads and the caring in their hearts to become women. This has been the way humans have survived for more years than I know. Not every man or every woman, mind you, but most have been taught to think like this."

"But Grandma, that means Stupid Stevie Silverman is supposed to be the boss of me, doesn't it?"

She pulls me close to her bony chest. I can smell the flowers in the special kind of powder that she uses every morning after her bath. Then she holds me at arms' length and says, "No, Ketzaleh. We all need to learn to think with our brains, hearts, and bodies. Girls need to grow up to lead, and boys to connect. Humans need to find ways to make possibilities from their differences. That's why Life made a one-of-a-kind Promise for each of us the moment we were born."

That's a lot for me to think about, but Grandma says, "Because you have your very first scar, I'm going to teach you how to light the candles."

I've wanted to do this since I was really little. Maybe she'll forget about the forgiveness stuff. But a question just blurts out of my mouth before I can stop it. "Have you forgiven the Cossacks, Grandma?"

She looks over at me, eyes shining as if they are made of dreams. "That's why we need Rosh Hashanah, Ketzaleh. It reminds each of us to clean our hearts so we can connect with one another, especially those who make dark shadows in the world."

Grandma doesn't realize that Stupid Stevie Silverman won't learn anything. She reaches for the matches and puts two candles in the silver holders. "So now, my darling, let me show you a ritual to help you learn how to understand and forgive Stevie and yourself at the very same time. It will grow your heart."

The excitement bubbles that had been in that heart sink down into my belly. But before I have a chance to resist, she continues.

"There are two candles on the table. They're partners to each other. The flame is like the Life Force. Let's pretend that one candle is you and one is Stevie. When you strike the match and touch it to the first wick, think about the Promise Life made to the world the moment you were born."

I strike the match on the rough side of the red box and then hold the flame to the wick. I think about how much I love to tell stories that connect people together.

"Now, move over and light the other candle, my darling. When you think of what Stevie did, think also of a time when you did something stupid that caused someone else to be hurt."

A memory rises immediately of when I crawled up on top of the mahogany bureau in my parent's bedroom and hid behind the big glass mirror. As soon as my sister Joan came in, I pushed it, and the mirror crashed down, breaking into a million pieces. One of them stuck into her arm and made blood squirt out. "But I didn't mean to, Grandma."

"Of course not, darling. You made a mistake. You're human, and humans always make mistakes. That's why we need to notice how those mistakes affect other people so we can learn from them and forgive ourselves. If we don't learn, we keep doing the same things over and over, pretending that what happened is someone else's fault." She strokes my curly red braids and continues quietly, "You can even remind the other person that they are bigger than their mistakes. Can you imagine saying that to Stevie?"

I rub my bandage and the new scar tissue that's growing under it. I imagine shouting at Stevie, "I know you're a better person than this, Stillman." My heart feels a little softer.

"Just so, Ketzaleh." She takes a second match out of the red box and hands it to me. I strike it and light the second candle. Grandma smiles and shows me how to move my hands in a special way, swooping them first into the shadows and then into the light, over my head, heart and belly like a dance. She whispers, "May we celebrate the light and learn from the shadows."

Finding My Unlived Parentheses

When Andy and I received an invitation to speak at a conference
dedicated to repairing the ruptures between men and women in
the world, we knew we had to go, in spite of the fact that India was
a very long way to travel. We flew to Rajasthan, where we were
picked up in a rusting rattletrap of a car by a perpetually smiling
man named Ullu. He chattered in Hindi as he raced over ruts
and potholes up the winding road to Mount Abu. At the top, he
screeched to a halt at a place called Peace Village, and both of us,
white-knuckled, began to breathe again.

Walking into the main meeting room, I was surprised to see twenty
glass booths surrounding the auditorium with a translator in each.
Over a hundred participants from more countries than I could
count were milling around, speaking languages I had never even
imagined. As we waited for the opening session, we were given
headsets to wear during the meetings so we could understand each
other. Then a plump silver-haired woman dressed in white with a
bright red dot in the middle of her forehead and iridescent brown
eyes was introduced as Dadi Janki. I was aware that she was the
first female head of a religion I had ever met. As the room settled in
silence, she began to speak. The translator in my ear said that she
was going to teach one phrase to connect us when we were away
from the translators in that room: "Om Shanti. May there be peace
within and between us."

As I climbed the stairs to the stage to address all those diverse
people with opening remarks to the conference, I had no idea what
was going to come out of my mouth. "Om Shanti." Everyone in the
room echoed back the words. Then, in a quivering voice, I began:
"Telling stories is my true native language. It has taken me many

years to realize that some of the stories we tell ourselves and each other limit possibilities, while others liberate them and allow us to love the lives we are living." My breath steadied. I went on to ask what I had come all that way to discover: "What are the stories and rituals that are helping the people in your country heal the ruptures and violence between men and women?"

A man from Bali told a story about how the people in his village used dance and art to express the most difficult of emotions and problems so they could be explored. He said they also hung symbols of those feelings—lust, jealousy, and rage—outside their houses. They made offerings of fruit and flowers to the demons. In this way, they recognized the existence of emotions that caused violence, but also acknowledged their intention to prevent it from entering their homes.

A woman from South Africa stood and told a story about how her family had healed the wounds of apartheid through the Truth and Reconciliation process. "It has given us a way to witness and speak directly to the perpetrators of the gross violence done. It provides the perpetrator the opportunity to mend the violation in public without fear of retribution or further damage."

Hours passed. Not one person spoke a word of blame or accusation. As we witnessed what could be possible, a river of tears and wonder began to carry and connect the whole community. I imagined all the women and men with whom Andy and I had worked who had suffered sexual violence floating in that river. I imagined those who stood behind us and those who would follow us—my son David, and all of the children of all the participants—being washed clean in the wisdom we had been sharing.

At the beginning of the closing session, I walked back on stage with Andy, wondering what story would rise from the fullness I felt. "We'd like to close this conference with our love story, because it illustrates the possibility of dignifying our differences. My experience tells me that this is one way we can save ourselves, through and with each other. I'll tell the story, and Andy will enact it to bring it alive."

Once upon a time, there was a large, muscular gander named Dummy. He only thought about how to enjoy the present moment by charming the many young feathered things that flocked around him. One day, a new goose named Nummy landed on the shore. Dummy, of course, made his approach and introduced himself, puffing out his chest so she would be duly impressed. Nummy ruffled her rather scraggly feathers and stuck her head under one wing. She told him in no uncertain words that she had more important things to think about.

Dummy was completely confused. What could be more important than sharing the present moment with his magnificent self? Nummy just sighed and explained that she was quite ill and needed to figure out how she could help create a world that all the young goslings yet to come could love. Dummy tilted his head one way and then the other as if rolling thoughts around. He told her that if she was so sick, it was only fair that she should experience a little love in this life now, before she left it. He declared that he'd be happy to help her do that. Nummy, touched in spite of herself, got so lost in her vision of what could be possible that she barely noticed Dummy's wing when it spread tenderly over her back or that the sky had turned to bronze— and so had her heart.

The next part of the story is so obvious that it barely needs telling. Dummy taught Nummy how to take pleasure in the moment, which led her to feel healthy and complete in a way she never had before. And as for Dummy, well, he realized that his passion for life was hollow without a sense of the Promise in him. He began to wonder what horizon he could reach for.

At this point, Nummy began to think. And when she did, she realized that although pleasuring in the moment was quite lovely, it did not help her mend the very tattered and torn world in which she lived. She also recognized that she only felt healthy and whole when she was tucked under Dummy's wing. If he ever left her, as he was prone to do, she'd be both bereft and unhealthier than ever. That made her notice things about Dummy that heretofore had been invisible. She accused him of wasting his time doing dumb things like surfing and whistling at all the young geese that waddled by.

Dummy was stung and stunned. He had felt so brilliant when her head was tucked under his wing. Now, he was carried away by the icy wind of her words and squawked that she wasted moments she could love thinking about all the things in the world that she didn't. A great rupture tore them apart. Nummy flew away to the north, and Dummy waddled along the shore flexing his wings and chasing every bit of fluffy tail he could find. But he felt a hole in his heart and found himself staring forlornly at the orange disk of the sun as it melted into the ocean. He began to wonder what the Promise inside him could be. Absentmindedly, he began to hum his questions and draw possibilities in the sand.

Meanwhile, without Dummy to make her feel whole and healthy, the pain in Nummy's body was so severe that she couldn't ignore it. She lay on her back, feeling exquisitely awkward, and began to roll, then stretch, then flex a muscle here, a tendon there. The more attention she gave to her body, the more it responded. She even began to strut, to prance, to dance with her eyes closed, feeling the music deep in her bones. Sometimes, though, when the moon was full and a star hung next to it, Nummy felt a hollow ache that went beyond words.

Several months later, Nummy saw a lone gander swimming toward her island. It was, of course, Dummy. He waddled up to her and shyly told her that he longed to sing to her the music in his heart and the ideas in his mind. He explained that he had remembered how as a young gander, his father had taught him that dreaming and imagining and caring about the feelings of anyone else would make him weak and a loser. He had therefore exiled that tender part of himself out of his mind. When Nummy left him, he had realized that he had to make a home for it, so he invited it to nest in the hole of his heart.

Dummy, with his voice quivering, asked if now that she didn't need him anymore, she still wanted to be with him. Nummy tilted her head one way and then the other before explaining that while she no longer needed him, it didn't mean she no longer wanted him. Now there was more of her to want than ever. She explained that she intended to memorize all the loving moments they had together, so that even if he was dumb enough to fly away, she'd have a heart full of enough loving memories to enjoy for a long time. Flying away from Nummy, however, was one thought that didn't enter Dummy's newly reclaimed mind.

As I write this, I don't remember how the conference actually ended. I do know that we left knowing that neither women alone nor men alone, nor one country nor any one leader can repair the ruptures that threaten us all. I did learn at Mount Abu that the Greek word for truth is "alitheia," which means "not to forget." I left Peace Village knowing that I would never forget that our differences, including the different ways we love and know and think, aren't the problem. Excluding any part of the darkness I see in others means losing access to the luminous wisdom that connects us all.

Even Here, Love Can Grow

I had quickly agreed to speak at the conference in Lindau, Germany. The woman on the phone who invited me had an elegant and magnetic voice. I was promoting my first book, *The Art of the Possible*, and an all-expenses paid honeymoon with Andy would be sweet.

It was late August when Mila picked us up in her white Mercedes at the Munich airport. Heading south, my inherited awkwardness at being a somewhat Jewish woman in Germany softened as we drove through deep pine forests that smelled dark green and passed placid shimmering lakes. While Andy slept in the back seat, Mila and I discovered that we had both been born in 1942. After several hours on the autobahn, we passed an exit sign that said "Dachau." The muscles and tendons in my body sprang tight, as if they were steel cables. Before I could even think, I heard myself say, "Here, let's stop here!" I couldn't believe I had said that. The three of us made our way silently, awkwardly, haltingly, through the concentration camp. Andy had never been to a camp before; I had been to Auschwitz with David, but this time the hungry ghosts of my family members who had been incinerated in Dachau shadowed every step.

We returned to the car, stunned. As we drove past the neighboring town, Mila pointed out the window to her right and said, "I spent the first four years of my life in that village." We were all so silent for the next two hours that I could hear my heart pounding against my ribs. Finally, she turned off the autobahn in Lindau, a resort town built around the shores of Lake Constans. Driving up to the main plaza in front of the conference center, the bubble of my surreal dream popped, and I focused on a banner stretched across the entrance with German words I couldn't read on it. I asked Mila what they said.

"Welcome to the 'Art of the Possible'!" she exclaimed.

"How strange. That's the title of my book!"

Mila placed her long slender fingers gently on my shoulder and said, "Of course, Dawna. This whole conference is about your book!"

I had thought I'd be doing one of many workshops at some small European psychology conference when I agreed to attend. After we unloaded the car and checked into our rooms, we went back down to the lobby, where several hundred people were entering the amphitheater. Within a few minutes, every seat was filled. Mila introduced the two translators who would be standing on either side of me: a thin blonde woman who would be bridging simultaneously from English to German and a tall lean dark-haired man who would bridge from German to English.

I climbed up the steps to the stage, wondering how to begin. I usually started a speech in a foreign country by greeting the participants in their native language, but I only knew one German phrase. As I stood behind the podium, it was as quiet inside my mind as it was in the room. I looked around at all the expectant faces and said "Danke sehr. Thank you. I'm embarrassed that's all I know how to say in your language. I grew up in a Jewish family where two aunts, one uncle, and several cousins died in Dachau. German was considered to be the language of the oppressors."

I paused long enough for the blonde woman translator to catch up with me. By the time she was finished, half the people in the room had folded their arms across their chests. Nonetheless, words continued to be pulled through me as if they were silk ribbons in a strong wind. "That was fifty years ago. My ancestors taught me that we had been victimized by your ancestors, and yet…and yet, as I look at your faces now, I realize that you came all the way here to listen to this fifty-year-old woman talk about her book, *The Art of the Possible*. I am truly in awe, lost in wonder."

Pausing again for the translation, tears began to roll down my cheeks. They became a river to carry the words that followed next. "Standing here today, I realize how incredibly difficult it must have been for you to grow up with *your* history. It truly is amazing that you came here to listen to me, to celebrate this book with me, to explore together what the real art of the possible can be fifty years after the Holocaust."

The translation stopped. Both the tall bony man and the thin blonde woman were silently crying and embracing each other. While the translators spilled out my words, I sat down on the edge of the stage. As I looked around the room, audience members leaned forward in their chairs, and then reached for one another, grasping hands. I stood up, placed my palms together and bowed, whispering, "Danke sehr." The male translator responded by saying "Ah shay-nem donk." I remembered that was "Thank you" in Yiddish. The woman said, "Merci beaucoup." Around the room people called out, "Grazie," "Dank u wel," "Arigato."

I asked people to form small groups of three or four and tell each other about those who had come before them, those friends and family members who had made it possible for them to be at the conference, and those who would follow them, the ones they wanted to pass on what they learned. Andy, Mila, and I clustered on the stage floor. She haltingly told a story about how her mother had to work during the war as a "paid girlfriend" to the Nazi soldiers in that small town we had passed outside Dachau so she could feed her two young daughters. She spoke of her own two fine sons and her first grandchild, who would be born later that spring. Time melted. I stood up and walked behind the podium as Andy taped huge sheets of white newsprint on all the walls and Mila passed around markers. I asked people to silently ask themselves the question, "What specifically do you want to learn while you are here so that those who follow you will experience the possibility of knowing how love their lives even in the shadow of rupture and ruin? Please write and/or draw whatever comes into your mind on the blank paper." Andy played versions of John Lennon's song, "Imagine," in five different languages over the sound system.

Fifteen minutes later, we all walked silently around the room reading what had been scrawled on the walls. I asked people to bring to mind those who came before them and those who would follow them so they could be present with us in that remarkable moment. Mila and the three translators climbed back onstage and sang "Imagine" in German:

Stell dir vor, es gibt den Himmel nicht,
Es ist ganz einfach, wenn du's nur versuchst.
Keine Hölle unter uns,
Über uns nur das Firmament.

The word "art" means the expression or application of human creative skill and imagination. The word "possible" means that which is within one's power or capacity to create. In Lindau, I discovered what I had truly come to find: Even in the darkest shadow that memory can hold, it is still possible for love to grow.

Will I Lose Everyone I Love?

My parents didn't talk about death in our house on Rugby Road.
I never attended a funeral. But there were mysterious days when
my mother and father wore black clothes. As far as I knew then,
people didn't die, they just disappeared: Mrs. McLean the landlady,
along with her dog Inky; Mr. Schwartz the butcher, who chopped
up chickens in the store on Ditmus Avenue and wore a bloody
white coat; and my very favorite, bestest Aunt Chuch. She was the
one with big cushy thighs that I used to snuggle into before going
to sleep so she could read me stories about Tom Sawyer and Huck
Finn, Alice in Wonderland, and Jo March and her sisters. She read
to me every night for the year she lived in our house. She even read
when she was sad because her husband, Uncle George, was mean
to her and made black and blue marks on her cheeks. Aunt Chuch
nestled me onto those thighs and, within a few minutes, we were
both absorbed into another time and place.

On the morning she disappeared, the sun was high in the sky, but
she still hadn't come out of the guest room. I opened the door just
a crack and tiptoed over to the single bed where she slept. The
fuzzy yellow blanket was pulled up right under her chin, but when I
touched her cheek with one finger, it was cold and blue. I shook her
shoulder just a little, but it didn't move. She was stiff all over, like
ice. I ran into my mother's room and told her about Aunt Chuch.
That made my mom behave very strangely. Before I could ask
anything, she picked up the black phone by her bed, began dialing,
and with her hand over the mouthpiece, told me to go walk Honey,
our cocker spaniel, and then go to my best friend Joycie's house. As
she began to talk to into the phone, Mommy pushed my shoulder
hard and told me to do what she said.

Later that evening, the Rabbi was in our living room. It was the first and last time he ever came to our house. I was surprised because I thought he lived in the temple, but there he was sitting on our couch, reading to my mother from a black book. Aunt Chuch was gone. I could hear his nasally voice mumbling something like "Yay. Walking through a valley of death with lots of shadows. I shall not be afraid of evil because a stiff rod is going to comfort me." It certainly wasn't the kind of story Aunt Chuch would have read. The words just made a jumble in my head. The next morning, Aunt Chuch's bed was empty. My parents were dressed in their black clothes. We all got in Daddy's new baby blue Buick and drove to Hell's Kitchen, where they dropped me off at the stoop in front of Grandma's apartment. I ran as fast as I could up the stairs. My favorite place to hide in Grandma's apartment is under the shiny red oilcloth covering the table where she chops vegetables and kneads golden bread dough. It hangs halfway down to the black and white checkered linoleum, making a perfect secret tent. It is a dark place where tears can flow without needing to be explained.

Grandma shuffles into the kitchen but doesn't say a word. She begins to sweep the drawers clean with a chicken feather. From my shadowy tent, I sob, "Grandma, where did Aunt Chuch go? Will I ever see her again?" I hear the sound of newspaper tearing, so I peek out. She is sitting on the maple rocking chair holding a long strip of torn paper across her lap. I watch her gnarled and nimble fingers turn the ends toward each other as if to make a circle. But then she makes one twist in the strip and joins the ends together with a sticky dab of dough. Decades later, I would learn that this is called a Möbius loop, but, to Grandma, it was a way to describe what couldn't be defined.

I am too curious to hide in the tent anymore. She takes my pointer finger and traces it round the outside of the loop. Whispering as if a mysterious secret is going to emerge, she says, "When your aunt was alive, she lived here, on the outside. Yesterday, she left her body. She died." Her floury hand guides my finger through the twisting place where the strip turns. She continues to move it. I'm very surprised to find that my finger is now on the inside of the loop. "When she left her body, Chuch moved here, inside your heart." Then Grandma slides my finger back up to the twist. "I call this the Meeting Place, because you can meet anyone you've loved here and bring them alive again. Think about your aunt. Then just do the thing you do so well: tell a story about her to someone else or write it down. When you do that…" She slides my finger until it is tracing the outside of the strip again, "…the story will bring her alive for you and the person hearing it. That's why telling stories is important, Ketzaleh. It makes it possible for what has been most precious to be reborn, again and again."

"But Grandma, how did she get there? Does everybody die? Will I lose everyone I love?"

She slides me up on her yellow-aproned lap and begins to rock slowly back and forth, back and forth. This always slows the questions down long enough for her to respond to them one at a time. "Being human, Ketzaleh, means that someday we will lose everyone and everything." Her warm hand comes to rest on my chest. "Each of us eventually will lose everyone and everything that's precious to us, at least on the outside. That's just the way life makes room to grow more. It's like a flower that dies to free its seeds."

She knows more questions are pressing against my lips, so she places a fingertip there gently and continues, "Remember how I told you about the Island of your Heart? When someone you love dies, you must plant the seeds, the things you love most about them and learned from them, on the Island in your Heart. They'll sprout in you. Then they'll blossom and maybe fruit out in the big world. That's one way their Promise can keep growing even after they're dead."

I get very, very, very quiet. This is a big thing to think about. I feel my mind turning it over and over the way my stomach does after swallowing a bite of her golden bread.

"That's why it's important to really enjoy what and who you love, to memorize them so the Promise seeds they've left can root deeply into this Island." She places her warm palm on the bony bump in the center of my chest.

I put my hand over hers. "Will your seeds live on the Island of my Heart too, Grandma?"

She takes my hand in hers and kisses the sweaty palm. "If you memorize these moments very well, they will. Then, maybe someday you'll tell them in stories or write about them in a book. That will make the seeds of my Promise and the seeds of your Promise blossom so they can be passed on to many others."

I imagine red and yellow tulips blooming in my chest. I know that Grandma's seeds will sprout right next to Aunt Chuch's. And even though she didn't say so, I know that I'm planted on the Island of each of their Hearts too.

Unlearning to Not Speak

I went to visit my mother in her South Florida condo for two weeks when she was the same age I am now. It was June 27, her birthday. It was also the birthday of my great-aunt Emma Goldman. But I didn't talk to my mother about Great-Aunt Emma. She would have had a fit. No one in her family spoke about Emma. Most families have someone or several someones they just don't talk about. There were some things about me—hair, eyes, voice, radical spirit that refused to be contained—that reminded my mother of Great-Aunt Emma. Her deepest fear was that I would turn out to be just like her.

Emma Goldman was a revolutionary born during the late 1800s. She was also an infamous anarchist who believed in the independence of women—their right to support themselves, live for themselves, and love whom they pleased. She believed in everyone's right to beautiful, radiant things. The words for which she was most often quoted were: "I represent truth and a never-to-be-destroyed longing for liberty… The ultimate success of a truth depends not on the many but the perseverance and earnestness of the few." Even as I write them now, these words don't seem very radical, but when I mentioned them once to my mother after seeing Robert Redford's movie about Emma, *Reds*, she reacted as if she wanted to strangle Emma and muzzle me.

In the 1930s, people could be deported, as Emma was, for words such as those. In the 1940s, they could be taken by train to Dachau, as many of our relatives were for saying those words. In the fifties, my parents and I watched Joe McCarthy on our tiny ten-inch screen television and heard people being humiliated, fired from their jobs, or exiled after saying words like these. Whenever I'd say something my mother considered to be radical, her jaw would tighten, then she'd shake her head and mumble, "You're going to end up just like your great-aunt Emma."

It was June 27, 1990, and I had come to Hollywood, Florida, to surprise my mother and make a fuss over her. I cooked her favorite matzo ball soup and roast chicken. Later, I ran a luxurious bubble bath sprinkled with Chanel #5, placed a candle near the tub, and laid out a fluffy towel and her favorite nightgown. Twenty minutes later, I went to kiss her good night and tuck her in bed. As I did so, I discovered that she was wearing a Playtex living girdle under that threadbare pink cotton nightie. For those of you who are fortunate enough never to have encountered a Playtex living girdle, let me describe it to you: it was a flat tube of flesh-colored rubber that held all movement and breath to a minimum. When I asked her why she was wearing that thing under her nightgown, she shrugged, played with the wide gold wedding band she still wore, and said sheepishly, "Being held in tight instead of being loose and free feels familiar. I've worn it every night for sixty years. I'm used to it. What would people think if I just hung out all over?"

I sighed. This was her mantra, "What would people think?" "But Ma, Dad's been dead for years. You're in bed alone. There's no one here now except you and me. No one will see you while you sleep."

"But maybe I'll have a heart attack and have to go to the hospital in the middle of the night like your father did and the ambulance drivers and nurses and doctors will see me."

I sighed again. As much as her mantra, "What will other people think?" had confined me growing up, her stubbornness could be as impenetrable as that Playtex girdle. After I kissed her forehead and turned off the light, I heard her mumble something. I tiptoed over to the bed she had slept in for six decades with my father and leaned

over to hear what she was saying. She looked up at me with her wide
Coca Cola brown eyes, and said, "I'm sorry. I was wrong."

It was the last thing she ever said to me. Within minutes, she
stopped breathing. I made sure she was buried in that Playtex girdle
right next to my father. A few days after the funeral, I was supposed
to give all of her clothes to Goodwill. I opened the top drawer of the
wooden highboy that held her nightgowns and underwear, then the
second drawer and the third. They were all filled with tissue paper
wrapped silk robes, lace-edged nightgowns, and hand-embroidered
camisoles that my sister and I had given her over the years. Not one
had ever been worn. In the bottom drawer, there was a little note
written in her spidery left-hand cursive: "Dawna, these are too good
for me. I'll do just fine with my old schmates. You enjoy them."

I am the same age now that she was then. I have thought long and
hard about what she was sorry for. Perhaps it was the Playtex living
girdle and all that it represented. Perhaps not being able to enjoy
the negligees. Perhaps she was apologizing for her insistence that
I should always care more about what other people thought than
about speaking out what was true and most meaningful to me the
way Great-Aunt Emma did. And perhaps, just perhaps, she wanted
me to use the last words she ever said to free myself from the legacy
of silence and confinement that had suffocated the Promise within
her. Perhaps she didn't want me to fail at being myself and living a
life I could love.

Tomorrow Is Not Promised

A tragedy can create a fault line on the Island of your Heart, breaking everything that happens into "before" and "after." Peris's death a few months ago split my life that way. To locate any event in my history, I now say to myself, "Oh, that was before she died," or "Oh, that was after she died." The fissure happened when tumors filled so much of her brain that they pushed this "mensch" right out of her body.

In Yiddish, there are a thousand ways to call someone a fool, but only one to describe a person who is the opposite: a mensch. A mensch lives true to what's deep in her bones. A mensch communicates really important things to the rest of us without ever sounding important. Some people give you their heartbreak as if it is a gift; a mensch receives yours that way. It's been two weeks since she lifted free from her body at four thirty in the morning. In India, they say that's the time when Heaven is closest to the Earth.

When I first saw Peris sitting against a wall in the Pittsburgh workshop that Andy and I were facilitating, she wore rimless glasses wrapped over her ears with clear plastic fishing wire. She'd been born with severe scoliosis of her spine and part of her jaw missing. This made it difficult for her to speak. Nonetheless, she'd learned several languages including Serbian and Croatian and had become a master of arbitrage for Westinghouse. In the group, when it was her turn to speak, she pushed the lenses of those ever-slipping glasses up the bridge of her nose and proceeded to tell us a hysterically funny story about her uncle Emil, whose eyeglasses were so covered with greasy fingerprints that he could barely see through them. Another person might have described him with disdain, but something akin to a grin crossed Peris's face, and her hands sculpted him out of the

air so that we too could see the simple beauty of his humanity the
way she did.

She went on to explain that many of her family roots were dug
into Croatia. She loved the multi-cultural reality of the former
Yugoslavia. The fighting was ripping her apart. Her eyes glistened
as if she were feeling compassion for every soft thing that walked
on the earth. She told us that she wanted to travel back there to
work with as many people as she could, especially the children in
both the Serbian and Croatian refugee camps. She had decided to
have surgery that would correct her mangled jawbone. "I need a
lot of support. I'm terrified to have the surgery, but I want to speak
clearly enough so that I can connect deeply with every person I
meet on both sides." When she talked about the surgical procedure,
it was as if a shadow had crossed the moon. She was terrified to go
through it alone.

I knelt down in front of her, placed my palms on her wet cheeks,
and then painted her jaw with them, whispering, "This mouth will
make violence obsolete." Andy came to sit behind her and began to
sing, "Listen, listen, listen to our hearts' song. We will never forget
you; we will never forsake you. Listen, listen, listen to our hearts'
song." The rest of the group encircled us and sang the simple chant
in harmony. Finally, all that could be heard in the room was the
sound of the thirty of us breathing together.

During the break, I placed a brass bowl in the center of the room
with a five-dollar bill in it. Andy had written, "We are here for you"
across the picture of Lincoln's head. By the time we returned, the
bowl was filled with currency, flowers, seashells, and notes, as well
as a small piece of paper with the words to the chant printed on it.
There wasn't enough money to pay for the surgery, of course, but
the bowl held exactly what she needed to go through the operation.

Months later, she quit her job, moved to Boston, and decided to start a nonprofit organization called World Reach. With our fingerprints on her heart, she raised enough money to go to both the Serbian and Croatian camps, bringing with her donated Polaroid cameras and shoes for the women so they would know they weren't alone. She told dirty jokes to them in both languages. She helped the children of each side take photographs, which she then put together into an exhibition that circled the globe entitled, *Eyes from the Storm*. Viewers of the exhibit wrote notes to the kids that she translated and took back to them on her next trip.

When Peris returned from her travels, she joined a training program we were teaching. I asked her to accompany us to a retreat center in Wisconsin that was also a Catholic convent. She enchanted the entire group with stories about the wounded refugees she had gifted with donated boots and sweaters. Her tales brought each one alive in the room. Those who had seemed so different at first become lovable and familiar, as if they were characters in our own families. She created a positive contagion. I found myself daydreaming about my wretched Uncle George and then the obnoxious braggart in a Dallas bar ten years earlier who had fallen off of a stool before throwing up all over me. After listening to Peris, I could think of them with humor and even warmth. I realized that each of the people I had made into enemies and thrown out of my heart represented an exiled aspect of myself, a need-in-disguise perhaps, that wanted to be reclaimed with curiosity and even wonder. Uncle George was a stand-in for my own untamed anger that needed to be educated, not rejected. The Dallas drunk was a replacement for my own need to be free from control every once in a while. With compassion, perhaps I could teach it how to be both free and safe.

That evening, after we had eaten in the large, cold cafeteria, Peris stood and pulled up the collar of her blue denim shirt. It was just like the kind her hero, Bruce Springsteen, might wear. The corners of her mouth twitched in a smile as she said, "This reminds me of a true story…" She proceeded to tell an outrageously filthy joke in English, Serbian, and Croatian. She continued telling dirty jokes for over ninety minutes without ever repeating herself. Unbeknownst to any of us, a group of fifteen chaste and pure nuns in white starched habits were hiding behind the big stone pillars that surrounded the dining room. We couldn't see them, but we certainly did hear them giggling. They were as beguiled by Peris's shining, bawdy innocence as the rest of us. In that moment, I wanted nothing more than to instantly manifest a bright purple T-shirt for her to wear emblazoned with the words, "All who are different belong. Love them nonetheless!"

Her humor has thumped me on the side of my numb head, bringing me into aliveness, for the past thirty years. Her gratitude and grace have salved my wounds and nudged me forward in the moments when all I wanted was to collapse into a muddled wet heap of dirty laundry. Her commitment to serving others inspires me to reach out in whatever ways I can, as she did. Peris was much shorter than I am. (Don't tell her I said that.) Once, when I patted her on the top of her head, she snarled, refusing to be diminished in any way. How did such a huge spirit ever fit in that small body and grow such a blessed resilience through physical challenges that would have crushed a person twice her size?

The way Peris died proves that nothing is fair and that Life is inherently precious and meant to be loved. The world is darker now than it has ever been. As I write these words, tears flutter out as if they were deep blue butterflies that had been trapped in a small jar in my chest. I wonder how this darkened world will ever shine again. As if in response to that question, her image rises in my heart. She is smiling, a fat unlit cigar hanging out of the left corner of her lips—those champion kissing lips—and a snifter of brandy in her right hand. When I am too weary to take a single step forward, I will ask, "What would Peris say? What would Peris do?" When I want to give up on everything and everyone, I will remember her fighting for her own agency during this long, lousy year when glioblastomas took up residency in her magnificent brain. I will remember the precious lesson she offered to me: "All who are different, belong. Love them, nonetheless."

Will You Ever Leave Me?

It is our last morning together, though I don't know that. It's early, and the city is still dark and mysterious. I am watching Grandma's big knuckled fingers braid her waist-length silver hair that's never been cut. It shines as if it has moon threads woven into it. Her bones seem luminous. Decades of learning and loving are sewn into the corners of her eyes. I ask her how she knows all that she does since she never went to school. She crosses one hank of hair over the other, exhales, pausing, and then crosses the third hank over the other two. She whispers to me, "I meet wise people here and there, in the market or the street, who share things with me as if we were members of the same family. I call them the Kindred." Another breath, in then out. Another pause. "And, of course, there are my prayers, which are really just wonders." As her fingers continue to plait the strands, her wondering mind does the same with problems and resources: "Evelyn's baby hasn't dropped yet. Mrs. Minsky gave birth easily to healthy twins last month. May Evelyn's birth be that smooth." Looking over her shoulder into the mirror on the wall, I can see the young face she must have had underneath the old one that is reflected there. I can see all of the Cossacks, and the babies that have died, all of her failures and fallings and risings again.

After we scramble out on the rusty orange fire escape, I snuggle under her arm and ask if she will hold me forever. She reaches into her yellow apron, pulls out a sticky sweet macaroon she made just for me that morning, and says, "Of course, Ketzaleh. You and I have found our way across the River into each other's lives, even if we don't know when or how we did it."

I'm confused. "What river, Grandma?"

"Why, the River of Life, of course!" She squints, looking out over the tenements of Hell's Kitchen as if she could see through the morning's muslin light to a place where there are rivers with banks that you can sit on and hillsides you can roll down. I take tiny mouse bites out of the cookie, not wanting to disturb her daydream with a question and not wanting to miss what tasted like the only food in a perfect world. The cookie lasts and lasts, but finally, after licking the last crumbs off my fingers, words fall out of my mouth.

"Grandma, there's this question I really need to ask you." I chew on the corner of my thumbnail, afraid that asking the question will make it so. She gently pries my hand open and kisses each fingertip as if reminding me that every question I have is worth asking. This gives me the courage to name what is hardest of all.

"Grandma, if I'm going to lose everything someday, will I lose you too?"

She tilts her head one way and then the other, as if she were a pigeon considering whether to fly off the ledge. She presses a warm cheek close against mine and whispers, "Can you find the one in your mind who wonders? Well, Ketzaleh, that's the same one who is listening to the words, questions, feelings, and thoughts that float through your mind. It's the one who is seeing the people down below us, tasting that cookie, and noticing how scared you are right now. Can you find that one, the one who is noticing and listening to the thoughts that whiz around?"

I nod and nibble, then decide I'd better check to make sure. "So what you're telling me, Grandma, is that all I have to do is wonder where that one is and it's right there."

"Just so, Ketzaleh. Now, here's something else to notice. When you look out through your eyes, there appears to be an oval window. Everyone else sees your face, but you see that oval window. Behind it, there is a wide endless darkness that seems to go on forever. I call it the Wonder Window. Can you find it?"

I blink and let my eyes get soft. Then I notice that there is an oval window instead of my face. Behind it and me is that darkness. Before I can ask another question, Grandma tells me to just breathe and imagine that all the people who came before me, all those who prayed that someday there would be one such as me, all those who passed their wisdom on to me, are in that darkness. They can see what I'm seeing, hear what I'm hearing, feel what I'm feeling. And the one who notices it all and wonders is back there, too.

I breathe slowly enough to find the space between the out breath and the in breath, the way she does. Soon everything gets wider and wider until it feels as if my mind spreads its wings. The questions stop and things lose their edges. The bells from St. Catherine's church down the street ring inside my whole body. I can feel the voices of the church choir under my skin.

Ever so slowly, Grandma presses her cheek against mine and then moves away. "There. Now. Find the Wonder Window on your own."

"But Grandma..."

She places a kiss on one of her fingertips and gently presses it to my quivering lips. I wonder who is the one smelling the pizza from Esposito's. I notice the oval that is my face and the darkness behind it. She whispers in my left ear, "You are always held by hidden hands. When I'm no longer next to you, I'll be behind you looking out through your Wonder Window, holding you as I am now with all the others who came before and passed seeds of their Promise on to you. As you get older and wiser, all the seeds planted on the Island of your Heart will sprout into blossoms, and then they'll fruit, which is what you are meant to pass on to others."

I feel her words as if they are a lullaby. She continues, "When you get caught up in the thoughts and stories in your mind, Ketzaleh, just step back into wonder, then find the one who is noticing that you are wondering. It's always been there. It never worries, never scolds, and is never angry. It will never leave you. This will always be so. After all, you can never lose who you really are. Your only job is to learn to love the life you are living and live a life you can love."

Grandma unfolds herself and walks carefully across the fire escape and through the open window of her apartment. I scramble behind, my heart beating, still afraid to be without her. I throw out one last question as if it were a lasso to hold on to her disappearing body.

"But Grandma, I'm still not sure what my Promise really is, or even who I can grow up to be or how I get the people who die to stand behind my Wonder Window."

She reaches her hand out to me and says, "The first two depend on which possibilities you choose to follow. As far as your last question…" She pauses for what seems like a long time, then says, "Just make sure that you tell people specifically how they matter to you. Not only when they are dying, but also when they are living. And remember to ask how you've mattered to them."

I put my hand in hers and she pulls me gently over the window ledge. Then, after straightening her yellow apron, she winks and says, "Well then, that's all you need to know!"

Grandma moved behind my Wonder Window the next week. She left that old, weary, and glorious body while I was sound asleep in a double-decker bunk bed at Camp Taconic. I never got the chance to tell her specifically how she had mattered to me. It's my one regret.

Giving What Only I Can Give

The known world shattered in the middle of my chest. The last
living member of my family of origin, my only sister Joan, was
diagnosed with a malignant tumor, a glioblastoma. It rapidly took
over most of the space in her brain. A few months earlier, she had
told me proudly that she never felt fear. "I just lock all those feelings
away someplace and never think about them again," she had said,
her left hand unconsciously gesturing toward the exact place in her
head where the first tumor was soon to emerge.

She was a proud and often rigid woman, unused to being dependent
on anyone. She was also used to being my seven-year-older sister,
the one in charge. When I was born, she wasn't happy to have her
place as Adored Only Child In The Family usurped. When I was
seven, she told me with all sincerity that I was adopted and really
didn't belong in our family. She proved her case by pointing out
how neat and organized she and my parents were, how precise and
procedural their minds were. Even her straight brown braids were
carefully aligned, whereas my hair was wild red, curly, refusing
to be constrained in any way, a perfect expression of the mind
underneath. I secretly believed that I was adopted for a decade until
my mother showed me my birth certificate. We had raging fights
throughout our childhood. She hated having to share everything
with her "baby sister," including our bedroom. One day she drew
a bright red lipstick line across the floor of our bedroom, declaring
I could not set foot on her side without asking permission. The
red line faded, but our differences divided us until the day she
was diagnosed.

I knew I couldn't help her in ways that would emphasize how
helpless she now was. Her illness challenged me to open my heart in

hell, over and over. I kept asking myself how broken apart in grief could become broken open in wonder. During the fifteen months of her illness, I shuttled back and forth from Northern California to Denver. Joan couldn't speak for most of that time. No longer overpowered by her authority, I finally got a chance to get a word in edgewise. I found every way I could to tell her very specifically how she had mattered to me. When we were kids, she had taught me to spell. Now I discovered that she could communicate by blinking while I spelled out the alphabet over and over to figure out what she wanted to communicate. The first full sentence she "said" to me in this way was, "When will this ugliness be over?"

One day, while sitting next to my helpless sister in her bedroom, I was wondering how I could make any kind of a difference. I thought of exiled author James Baldwin in Paris saying, "Not everything that can be faced can be changed. But nothing can be changed that cannot be faced." A ribbon of stories began to unfurl through my mind. I wrapped them around her: the time on Rugby Road in Brooklyn that we painted the landlady's dog Inky a shocking pink; spying on the showgirls who danced for Xavier Cuggat when we lived at the Edgewater Beach Hotel in Chicago; figuring out together how to breastfeed her first son Tommy in her Eastchester, New York, bedroom; learning to make the corn bread stuffing for the Thanksgiving dinner we prepared for our parents; learning to translate what she needed into Spanish when she gave birth to her youngest son Jimmy in a Puerto Rican hospital. In the long dark nights that I sat at her bedside, I wrapped our tattered history around us both by telling her these stories as if it were a beige cashmere shawl.

Embedded in each story was a message about all the things she had taught me: the inspiration of beauty in the world; taking delight in the differences in people, which she had discovered when traveling all over the globe with her beloved husband Lew. I reminded her of the first time I had ever seen her inspired by art. It was also the first time I realized how different we were. She was fifteen years old and in full bloom. She decided to take me on a train trip to New York City so I could see real paintings in the Metropolitan Museum. At the end of the day, too exhausted to walk anymore, we collapsed on the wide, granite steps next to the big concrete lions in front of the building on Fifth Avenue. We sat there for an hour. More people walked by than I had ever seen in my whole life. I was fascinated that never, ever, did I see two who looked the same. On the train ride home, all I could talk about was all those people and how each one of them had a different story, history, and possible future. All Joan could talk about was the color, light, lines, textures, and style in the paintings and sculptures that hung in those big drafty rooms. I had never seen her so alive.

Here we were five decades later, she in a hospital bed after surgery to remove the first tumor, surrounded by the sound of never-ending soap operas and baseball games from the televisions hung on the walls around us. I tied tiny red ribbons into her few remaining strands of hair and painted her toenails Cherries-in-the-Snow, the color of the lipstick line she had drawn in our childhood bedroom. Sometimes I just sat silently on the ugly turquoise plastic chair next to her bed, touching her struggling body as it died. My heart stretched open the way she used to stretch her arms open so I could slide down into them at the playground on Ditmus Avenue. I lent her the strength of my body and mind while remembering how at sixteen, she had lent me her favorite white cashmere cardigan because I was shivering. I did whatever I could to love her the best I knew how so she would remember how to love herself.

When she finally was released from that ugly place, she returned to her impeccable postmodern home in Denver. My brother-in-law had set it all up like a small hospital, compete with full-time nurses who connected her to a feeding tube. The last time I visited and saw her lying there, completely helpless, I knew I had to do something to express my gratitude for all she had given to me. Words would not be sufficient. Sitting next to her while a nurse washed her body, I began to wonder. I remembered my Grandma and how much she had expressed through the ritual of preparing food for those she loved, and an idea emerged.

When we were kids, on very special occasions, my father used to take us to Lundy's restaurant in the Sheepshead Bay section of Brooklyn. After the waiter tied big white paper bibs around our necks, we devoured every buttery succulence that we could pry from the deep red orange shells of the two-pound lobster we shared. She always gave me the last bite. I decided to drive Joan's car to the local Safeway. I bought and boiled a two-pound Maine lobster and chilled a bottle of her favorite chardonnay wine. I returned to her impeccable kitchen and prepared a lobster feast, complete with melted butter, lemon slices, and a sleek crystal goblet full to the brim with Kistler chardonnay. I set it all out on a tray and carried it into the room where she lay in a rented bed, closed in by metal rails. I pushed a button on the bed's controls, raised her up into a sitting position, and tied a napkin over her nightgown and the feeding tube.

I dipped a large piece of claw meat very slowly into melted butter and ran it across her lips. I followed that by running my finger, dipped in cold white wine, over them. Even though she couldn't chew or swallow, I knew that she could still taste. While she watched, I threw the rest of the lobster and the bottle of Kistler very deliberately into the garbage can by her bed so that at the last, she wouldn't have to share something she loved with me anymore.

When I removed the napkin, she blinked the words "Thanks. I love you too. Now go home."

The next morning, as I stared out of the round airplane window on my flight from Denver to Salt Lake City, I knew that I was not only letting go of my sister, but also an important part of who I had been: no longer the youngest daughter, no longer the youngest sister.
But I wasn't an orphan either. After decades of living on the other side of the great divide of our differences, Joan moved behind my Wonder Window, where she still teaches me how to be inspired by the beauty in the world.

What Are You Waiting For?

Suzanna Takata, my "Dizzy Sister," and I were talking story and eating gazpacho on my lanai. I'd better explain. In Hawaii, where we live, people tend to talk in long ribbons of stories rather than short clipped Q and A East Coast sentences or loopy rambling West Coast phrases. A lanai would be called a porch in Brooklyn or a patio in California. And as for gazpacho, well, you probably know what gazpacho is by now. I call Suzanna and I "Dizzy Sisters" not because we are confused and disorganized and not because we are blood sisters. We both are frequently dizzy because of something we each struggle with called Meniere's disease. In the midst of a Meniere's episode, the world turns into a large bowl of shifting, spinning green Jell-O. Both Suzanna and I have lost most of the hearing in our left ears and some of our stability. Various doctors have told us that it's the result of an ear's inability to create balance. (My own hypothesis is that my left ear filled up with the tears that gathered over years of listening to so many people's suffering. It's now asking me to give attention to the internal guidance that's trying to come through. Suzanna thinks her left ear has been filled up with her aging mother's bitter tears. Doctors, of course, just roll their eyes at these possibilities and prescribe each of us Prednisone, diuretics, and a no-salt diet.)

Back to Dizzy Sister and I talking story and eating gazpacho. She told me she had to move her mother into her home because residential treatment for dementia was just too expensive. Suzanna had been looking forward to retirement, but now she was a full-time cook and caregiver. (Are women ever *not* full-time cooks and caregivers, we pondered together?) Her mother refused to eat unless coerced. She had lost a great deal of weight because her hunger response had disappeared. So had her hearing. "She can still complain though! And she does, endlessly, about everything I try to do for her!"

Suzanna's jaw clamped so tightly that the tears, which had risen to the rims of her eyes, couldn't fall. "Somewhere along the way, my mother has lost her ability to express and receive love to me. I'm afraid I'm losing mine as well!"

I asked Suzanna whether she had written a letter to her mother telling her the specific ways she mattered. She shook her head, took another long sip of tea, looked up at me through wet black eyelashes, and artfully changed the subject. "Enough about me, Dawna. How are your 'episodes'? Have you found something that helps?"

I knew I couldn't give her therapeutic guidance in the ways I used to when I was in private practice. Instead I began to talk story about my current fascination with pottery, which I'd been studying two nights a week at the nearby arts center. "My sister Joan was supposed to be the creative one in our family, and I was supposed to be the smart one. While she was alive, I avoided artsy things lest I make her even more jealous than she had been since the moment I was born. But since she's now dead, and since I've been spending so much time with spinning in my head, I figured that learning how to center clay on a spinning wheel in front of me might teach me how to relate to what's going on inside. At first, I came home from classes late at night disappointed, frustrated, annoyed, and filthy. I told myself I was wasting the too few remaining hours of my life engaged in what felt like a useless hobby. But, after four months, I can now plop a large white lump of clay on a spinning metal wheel and center it—most of the time."

The pupils of Suzanna's deep brown eyes were dilated, and her facial muscles had relaxed. She encouraged me to go on. "The amazing thing is that I never get dizzy in the studio. The clay is a remarkable mirror that shows me how I can relate to anybody or anything, even a dizzy episode, instead of being taken over by it. I'm learning to let go gently, to stay present and apply just the right amount of pressure, to open my mind as I open the clay. During the drive home, I sense that I'm really also learning how to relate to everything, including the challenges from the blank page of the book I'm writing. While my hands are shaping those lumps of clay, some part of my mind is exploring what really matters to me and how I can love the life I am living as it is. When the clay is leather hard, my fingers carve away everything that is not beautiful. Maybe this ceramics thing is all an unconscious plot to avoid writing or working out at the gym. All I know is that I'm definitely hooked."

Suzanna put her elbows on the table and rested her chin in her hands. "Why do you think that this is so important to you now?"

"Even at seventy-five, I still love being a beginner. When I was in private practice, each person I worked with was also an opportunity to be a beginner. The clay reminds me that life is really a perpetual apprenticeship in listening deeply enough to connect with myself or someone else in the most loving way possible."

I looked up at Suzanna, wondering how she was receiving what I was saying. She nodded slowly, so I risked a question. "I'm wondering. If your mother were a lump of clay on a spinning wheel in front of you, and you placed both your hands silently on her, what would they tell you is really going on for her right now?"

Suzanna closed her eyes, took a long slow breath, and then whispered, "She just wants to die so she can see my father. But she's terrified of dying because she doesn't know what it will be like to lose control that way. So she feels broken in two."

I reached out and held her hands between mine for several breaths, and then I asked her to wait while I went into my office to get two things I wanted to give her. I printed out a story I had written and grabbed a special clay bowl I'd made. Suzanna got up and started washing the lunch dishes.

I put the small black bowl in her hands. It had been broken in half. The pieces had been rejoined with glue and gold dust. I explained that it had been made whole again using a traditional Japanese art form called "kintsugi" which creates beauty in broken places by mending the cracks with lacquer and gold. Rather than trying to disguise it or cover it up, the damage is incorporated into its new form and increases its value and beauty immensely.

I put the folded paper I had printed out into the bowl and told her that it was for her mother to read, but that I wanted her ears to hear me read it to her first. I unfolded the paper and read the story out loud:

Let me tell you what dying feels like. Imagine an ice cube melting, then evaporating. Imagine you are the ice cube. A drop of rain falls into the ocean and becomes part of a swelling wave. Imagine you are the raindrop. A hand grabs so tightly onto something for decades that it becomes numb, and then finally it just releases open with a sigh. Imagine you are the hand.

I don't know how else to describe what it felt like for me to die. But decades later, I still am compelled to tell the story of how it happened: I was on an operating table. Or my body was. I heard the doctor yell to the nurse, "Damn! We lost her. Adrenaline, stat!" Then I felt as if I were falling upwards out of my body. It was a lot like falling in love or falling out of fear, falling through the clearest water you can imagine. All the nouns of identity dissolved in an instant, along with hope and horror. No more "mother," "sister," "friend." No more dissonance, fragmentation, or feeling pulled apart. Just a soul in wonder. I didn't see a light. My experience was more like being stained with light.

And since every truth must balance with another, I also experienced a profound darkness as I realized how incomplete my loving had been, how I had limited it with stories in my mind that had told me loving was a thing, a commodity I had to earn. I recognized how much my son would suffer as a result of the limited ways I had realized my love for him. My heart broke wide open—wide enough so there could be a conversation between the Light and the Life I had lived. It was subtler than thought, more like a whisper between a tree and the wind blowing through it.

"Have you had enough joy?"

"Enough joy? I haven't even begun to live, and now I've died!" (Even in a sacred moment, I was complaining of not getting enough!)

"Well, what have you been you waiting for?"

What could I say? These questions did not demand answers. All they required was that I open to them, hold them the way a bowl holds pure water. I fell back into my body, which was being wheeled on a gurney to the morgue. I would now say that I, who had never failed a test, flunked dying, except that as I slammed into my body, I realized that death is not a failure.

There is no end to this story. Ultimately, all I know is that you can't get rid of pain, fear, or suffering. You just have to practice touching them with tenderness and caring. Most important of all, what dying taught me is that I need to remember what really matters while living in wide-open wonder about the possibilities that life is presenting to me with each challenge. Even more than that, I have to love the moments that are available to me.

As Suzanna rose to leave, she reached for my hands and placed kisses into my palms. There was nothing else that needed saying.

Baking and Sharing

66

"If we all speak our truth, no matter how heavy or how trivial our stories seem, then together we can light the way toward a new future and a new story, one that is no longer based on silence and shame… Whenever we tell our truth and break our silence, we become like candles that light the way for others out of their darkness until they find the courage to speak up themselves."

—Zainab Salbi, ***Freedom Is an Inside Job***

What Would It Take to Let Go of the Forgetting of Joy?

My father was my tiny grandmother's youngest son. He towered over her at six foot three inches, with broad shoulders and a charismatic, dominating nature. His big secret was that he was functionally illiterate because he had to drop out of school in eighth grade to take care of his family after his father died. Nonetheless, he climbed the proverbial ladder of success from the slums of Hell's Kitchen in New York City to become the CEO of Hiram Walker Incorporated in Chicago because he could sell anyone anything. I secretly read all of his important papers into a big tape recorder every day after school. Late at night, he memorized it all by ear. People would follow him over the horizon if he asked them to because of his two strategies for success: 1) Never accept another person's limitations, no matter how firmly they believe in them. 2) Enter another person's model of the world and find the leverage there to make change possible.

After he retired, the company spit him out like overchewed bubble gum. He was lost and never found himself again. He and my mother sold their house in New England and retired to a condominium in Hollywood, Florida. In their case, I use the word "re-tire" literally, because they both suffered from the exhaustion of making it through the Depression and the second World War while raising two daughters as well as sustaining many of their siblings. As I rang the doorbell to visit them, I smiled at two words that were written on the doormat: "At Last!" I was there because a few months before, he had been diagnosed with Alzheimer's disease. I suspected it was going to be my last chance.

I was stunned when I saw him. That great lion had melted, dissolved, disintegrated. His once-fierce blue eyes were red and watery, staring off into some horizon I couldn't see. He was locked behind walls I couldn't climb.

When I was a child, he never said "I love you" because he was afraid it would weaken me in some way. Instead, he would always wink and slip me a quarter after I read his papers into the recorder and whisper, "Don't tell your mother."As a woman, I wanted more than anything for him to know *I* loved *him.* So when I was about to leave the condominium that day, I knelt in front of him and said, "I love you, Daddy." But my words bounced off of those invisible walls. I stood, slipped my purse over my shoulder, and then had an idea. I reached into my wallet, pulled out a five-dollar bill, opened his limp hand, and put the bill on his open palm. "Here's five dollars, Daddy, don't tell Mommy." He blinked and then blinked again. Looking straight at me, he said in a clear voice, "I love you too, sweetheart." It was both the first and last time I ever heard those words from him.

Several months later, he died with a shrug. The love I felt for him poured through me, a trickle at first, then a torrent. I did the only thing I knew how to do and turned my grief into ink. At three o'clock on a wintery Vermont night, I wrote a poem, more anthem than requiem. The first line was, *"I will not die an unlived life."* The next, *"I will not live in fear of falling or catching fire."* My hand and heart rushed to write the next line, *"I choose to inhabit my days, to allow my living to open me, to make me less afraid, more accessible; to loosen my heart until it becomes a wing, a torch, a promise. I choose to risk my significance, to live so that which came to me as seed goes on to the next as blossom, and that which came to me as blossom, goes on as fruit."*

To my surprise, six months later, it was published on the back cover of a book I wrote with the same title. Since then, that poem has been translated into more languages than I can count. People I've never met have posted, danced, and composed an overture to it. It has been made into greeting cards and paintings. Apparent strangers tell me a copy of it has been hanging over their desks for years, inspiring them forward. The seeds he planted have indeed gone on to blossom in me and through me as fruit.

I used to think that in order to really matter, a person would have to have a book on the Bestseller List, or receive the Nobel Peace Prize, run an organization of thousands, appear on the front page of the *New York Times*, or at the very least, be interviewed by a comedian on a major late-night television program. I'm too old and weary for any of that now. Perhaps you have your own secret criteria for proving that you really matter so that you can then love the life you are living.

In the moments when pieces of Humpty Dumpty lie shattered around my feet and all my efforts to repair what has been ruptured seem futile, when the slimy question, "Why bother?" causes my chest to cave in, my heart to sink, and my shoulders to slump, there's only one thing that really seems to make a difference. I step back, remembering the one in me who Knows, and give my attention to the following luscious open questions: What's unfinished for me to give, learn, and experience? Have I loved as many of the moments I was given as possible?

A month ago, a publisher told me that there are more people writing books now than ever before, but that fewer people than ever are reading books. I hung up the phone, and the dirge of "Why have I bothered?" began to echo in the chambers of my heart. I curled up on the couch with my tattered journal and my favorite blue

fountain pen and wrote that question at the top of the page. Staring
at the horizon, my hand, as if guided by my grandmother, began to
scribble the following words:

I have lived a loved life.
I no longer belittle my mind
or limit my heart.
I can stand calm in a wide moment
between sky that lifts me and gravity that grounds me.
I have let loving unfurl me,
then give me away.
I remember
I am nest,
harbor,
garden.
I pass Life forward
so that which came from those before me,
and that which grows in those next to me,
goes on to those who will follow me.

As soon as I laid the blue pen down, I looked around and saw three
wide-open hibiscus blossoms the color of a sunrise. I heard Java
sparrows twittering at the feeders and felt the same breeze touch me
that was making the palm fronds at the bottom of the hill dance.
What would my grandmother think of this place where I live? We
moved to the Hawaiian Islands because Andy had always wanted to
live near the ocean and play music with others and David and Angie
wanted to visit somewhere they could kitesurf. We came because I
heard that the inhabitants of these islands form close communities
called 'ohanas. I discovered that on weekends, many 'ohanas camp
on the beach and ask each other open questions, then other people
respond in talkstory. I learned that traditionally, when a person
dies here, those in the 'ohana gather around, lean over, and wait

to inhale his or her last *ha*, their breath of Life, spirit. In that way, it can be carried forward by the rest of the ʻohana. Learning all of this made it obvious that this was a place where we could live the life we love.

I am wishing now that you will become part of my ʻohana. I am wanting you to breathe in whatever *ha* you have found in these pages. I am fervently hoping that you will gather with others in your ʻohana of family, friends, acquaintances and ask some wide-open questions, making time for each of you to talkstory, share your own zavaʼah, and awaken the wisdom that will enable you to live a life you can love.

May you love the great Life you have been given fiercely and tenderly. May the unique Promise you carry within you rise, be braided, kneaded, baked, and shared. May it bless our hungry, frightened world.

Open Questions to Evoke "Talkstory"

What has made you feel fully alive?

Who and what has been easy for you to love?

What are you serving?

When have you taken a great personal risk that moved you forward?

What major challenges have grown you as a person?

Who has inspired you?

Who has blessed your future?

Who have you inspired?

Who and what has steadied you and made you feel safe?

When have you loved the moments you were living?

What's one thing that has been right about something that was wrong in your life?

Whose lives specifically have you touched?

What are the conditions that bring out the best in you?

What are you longing for?

When have you felt the Promise during a major challenge?

How have you related effectively to the things you can't control?

Appreciations

I know of no practice that has been as profoundly significant in teaching me how to love the life I am living than that of giving appreciations. I insist of myself that I do it before my feet hit the floor every morning, at the end of every session I do with someone, and when I nestle my head in the pillow and click out the lights. My "guidelines" are that they must be specific, believable, and true.

To those who came before me:

Grandma—for coauthoring this book with me, kissing my fingertips instead of pinching my cheeks, and planting a garden of seeds on the Island of my Heart right from the beginning.

Emma Goldman—for reminding me that love is free.

William C. Mechanic—for seeding me into life and teaching me to lead, and for your last lesson.

Edith Cohen Mechanic—for loving me in such a way that I knew it was true and for your last words.

Joan Sapiro—for teaching me most of what I know about both sides of generosity.

Aunt Chuch—for teaching me to love the written word and giving me the enchantment of stories.

Milton Erickson, MD—for teaching me to enter another's model of the world.

Bash Nola—for teaching me it's never too late to learn.

To those who stand next to me:

Andy Bryner—for helping me know that everything is a verb, and that "no matter what" is an anthem.

Brenda Knight—for midwifing this book and believing the world needs it.

Mary Jane Ryan—for standing behind me, page after page.

Joan Selix Berman, Colleen Sotomayer Mayeda, Lorraine Tamarabuchi, Sally Reed, Janet Cooper—for yeasting my life on this Island.

Luana—for reminding me again, again and again how necessary it is to reach.

Ed Enomoto and Jill Getzan—for teaching me that beauty can grow through my hands.

Suzy Amis Cameron—for learning and teaching how to trust ourselves more deeply as Evolutionaries.

Al Carey—for the lessons about inspiration and generosity.

Joyce Chin—for the passionate inspiration to love the way I see the world.

Georgi Abelanda—for listening so much of this into speech while helping my body learn how strong it can be.

Harmony Hallas—for catching me when I fall and catching every detail when it drops.

Pat Dunn—for teaching me what brothering could be like and reminding me about simple attention.

Karin Reimpell—for helping me learn to experience grace as a verb.

Chris McKenney, Robin Miller, Michelle Lewy, Hannah Jorsted Paulsen, Merritt Smail, Natasha Vera, and Hugo Villabona, for saying the sweetest words I could ever hear: "Yes. How can we help?"

A. Leslie Noble, a.k.a. Michaleangelina for editing away everything that was not elephant in such a caring and impeccable way.

Joyce Stillman Meyers—for traveling from Rugby Road to Crayon Land and believing in the enchantment of my stories.

To those who will go on after me:

David Adam Peck—You edited all but one of the stories in this book, checking form and clarity, including the ones that were difficult for you to read. Like Rumpelstiltskin in reverse, you have brought my loving down to earth and insisted I live it for as many minutes as possible without forgetting about the joy of leaping.

Angie McArthur—You teach me again and again how powerful and graceful inquiry can be when it comes through both heart and mind. Without knowing, I prayed that someday I would have you to follow and lead me.

Makena Jost—You have taught me that it is never necessary to stoop and always a gift to bow with respect. I will always follow your footsteps.

Finn Grace Li—You have taught me how to be fervently loyal to my questions, and that my heart can follow my hands.

Bibliography

Berry, Thomas. *The Great Work: Our Way into the Future.* New York: Harmony/Bell Tower, 1999.

Didion, Joan. *Slouching Towards Bethlehem.* New York: Dell, 1968.

Erickson, Milton H., MD, Rossi, Ernest L. *Experiencing Hypnosis: Therapeutic Approaches to Altered States.* New York: Irvington, 1981.

Feldenkrais, Moshe. *Awareness Through Movement.* New York: Harper One, 1990.

Frankl, Viktor E. *Man's Search for Meaning: The Classic Tribute to Hope from the Holocaust.* London: Rider, 2001.

Galwey, Timothy. *The Inner Game of Work: Focus, Learning, Pleasure, and Mobility in the Workplace.* New York: Random House, 1999.

Kaur, Valerie, "3 Lessons of Revolutionary Love in a Time of Rage." Ted.com, Feb. 8, 2018.

Macy, Joanna. *Active Hope: How to Face the Mess We're In without Going Crazy.* Novato: New World, 2012.

Markova, Dawna, PhD. *I Will Not Die an Unlived Life: Reclaiming Purpose and Passion.* Berkeley: Conari Press, 2000.

_____. *Random Acts of Kindness.* Berkeley: Conari, 1993.

_____. *Kids' Random Acts of Kindness.* Berkeley: Conari, 1994.

_____. *No Enemies Within: A Creative Process for Discovering What's Right About What's Wrong.* Berkeley: Conari Press, 1994.

_____. *Spot of Grace: Remarkable Stories of How You* Do *Make a Difference.* Novato: New World Library, 2008.

_____. *Wide Open: On Living with Passion and Purpose.* Berkeley: 2008.

Palmer, Parker. *On the Brink of Everything: Grace, Gravity, and Getting Old.* Oakland: Berrett-Kohler, 2018.

Remen, Rachel Naomi, M.D. *Kitchen Table Wisdom: Stories That Heal.* New York: Riverhead Books, 1996.

Salbi, Zainab, *Freedom Is an Inside Job: Owning Our Darkness and Our Light to Heal Ourselves and the World.* Boulder: Sounds True, 2018.

Author's Note

"Stories are our nearest and dearest way
of understanding our lives and finding our
way onward."

—**Ursula LeGuin**

All of the stories in this book have grown out of my life experience. In that sense, all are true, but all may not be factual. I have attempted to attribute those stories which came to me from others to their sources, but some have been passed from person to person over decades and centuries, and in those cases, it is not possible to say where they originated. I have spoken and written some of the stories in this book in other forms in previous books and public forums. Many of the people's names and specific identifying characteristics have been changed to respect their privacy, and some are composites.

About the Author

Dawna Markova followed her precious grandmother's footsteps to become a midwife, but, rather than babies, she helps birth possibilities within and between people. She has lived many incarnations in the past seven decades as an author, teacher, psychotherapist, researcher, executive advisor, and organizational fairy godmother.

One of the creators of the bestselling Random Acts of Kindness series, Dawna is the author of many other inspirational books, including: *I Will Not Die an Unlived Life: Reclaiming Purpose and Passion*; *Reconcilable Differences: Connecting in a Disconnected World*; *Collaborative Intelligence: Thinking with People Who Think Differently*; and *A Spot of Grace: Remarkable Stories of How You DO Make a Difference.*

In her newest book, *Living a Loved Life: Awakening Wisdom Through Stories of Inspiration, Challenge and Possibility*, Dr. Dawna Markova braids together inspiring stories drawn from her precious grandmother's wisdom, her own life challenges and from the thousands of people with whom she has worked. In this fragmented Humpty Dumpty time, when all the king's horses and all the king's men are trying to convince so many that they really don't and can't make a difference, she asked herself three evocative questions to find and follow her own wisdom: How do I find a way to live a life I can love now? How do I help make it possible for those who will come after me to do the same? How do I re-collect the wisdom earned through my own and others' challenges? She explains, "Grandma taught me that there is wisdom hidden in your greatest difficulties. It can help you realize how you matter as well as what really matters to you. This is the essence of living a life you can love."

Mango Publishing, established in 2014, publishes an eclectic list of books by diverse authors—both new and established voices—on topics ranging from business, personal growth, women's empowerment, LGBTQ studies, health, and spirituality to history, popular culture, time management, decluttering, lifestyle, mental wellness, aging, and sustainable living. We were recently named 2019's #1 fastest growing independent publisher by *Publishers Weekly*. Our success is driven by our main goal, which is to publish high quality books that will entertain readers as well as make a positive difference in their lives.

Our readers are our most important resource; we value your input, suggestions, and ideas. We'd love to hear from you—after all, we are publishing books for you!

Please stay in touch with us and follow us at:

Facebook: Mango Publishing
Twitter: @MangoPublishing
Instagram: @MangoPublishing
LinkedIn: Mango Publishing
Pinterest: Mango Publishing

Sign up for our newsletter at
www.mango.bz and receive a free book!

Join us on Mango's journey to reinvent publishing,
one book at a time.